Basic accounting 2

Tutorial

David Cox

Michael Fardon

osborne
BOOKS

Published by Osborne Books Limited
Unit 1B Everoak Estate
Bromyard Road
Worcester WR2 5HP
Tel 01905 748071
Email books@osbornebooks.co.uk
Website www.osbornebooks.co.uk

Design by Laura Ingham
Cover and page design image © Istockphoto.com/Petrovich9

Printed by CPI Antony Rowe Limited, Chippenham

British Library Cataloguing in Publication Data
A catalogue record for this book is available from the British Library

ISBN 978 1905777 259

Contents

Acknowledgements

The publisher wishes to thank the following for their help with the reading and production of the book: Maz Loton, Cathy Turner and Jean Cox. Thanks are also due to Roger Petheram for his technical editorial work and to Laura Ingham for her designs for this series.

The publisher is indebted to the Association of Accounting Technicians for its help and advice to our authors and editors during the preparation of this text.

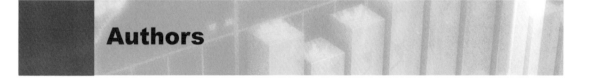

Authors

David Cox has more than twenty years' experience teaching accountancy students over a wide range of levels. Formerly with the Management and Professional Studies Department at Worcester College of Technology, he now lectures on a freelance basis and carries out educational consultancy work in accountancy studies. He is author and joint author of a number of textbooks in the areas of accounting, finance and banking.

Michael Fardon has extensive teaching experience of a wide range of banking, business and accountancy courses at Worcester College of Technology. He now specialises in writing business and financial texts and is General Editor at Osborne Books. He is also an educational consultant and has worked extensively in the areas of vocational business curriculum development.

Introduction

what this book covers

This book has been written specifically to cover Learning Area 'Basic Accounting II' which combines five QCF Units in the AAT Level 2 Certificate in Accounting:

- Maintaining and reconciling the cash book
- Banking procedures
- Maintaining petty cash records
- Maintaining the journal
- Maintaining control accounts

The book contains a clear text with worked examples and case studies, chapter summaries and key terms to help with revision. Each chapter has a wide range of activities, many in the style of the computer-based assessments used by AAT.

This book covers the areas of cash book, petty cash book, control accounts, journals and trial balance adjustments. AAT has recommended that the Learning Area 'Basic Accounting I' which covers the areas of financial documents and the theory and practice of double-entry should be covered before 'Basic Accounting II.'

Downloadable blank documents for use with this text are available in the Resources section of www.osbornebooks.co.uk

Osborne Workbooks

Osborne Workbooks contain practice material which helps students achieve success in their assessments. *Basic Accounting 2 Workbook* contains a number of paper-based 'fill in' practice exams in the style of the computer-based assessment. Please telephone the Osborne Books Sales Office on 01905 748071 for details of mail ordering, or visit the 24-hour online shop at www.osbornebooks.co.uk

International Accounting Standards (IAS) terminology

In this book the terms set out below are quoted as follows when they first appear in a chapter (and elsewhere where it seems appropriate):

IAS terminology (UK terminology), ie

receivables (debtors)

payables (creditors)

inventory (stock)

1 Introduction to banking procedures

this chapter covers...

This chapter is an introduction to the way in which payment systems operate within the banks and building societies in the UK.

Payment systems feature prominently in a study of book-keeping:

- *businesses receive payments from customers for goods and services sold*

- *businesses need to make payments to suppliers for goods and services sold*

- *businesses need to pay their employees*

We will deal with the recording of these transactions in the accounting system in later chapters. In this chapter we describe:

- *the main services offered by the banks and building societies*

- *forms of payment and their various clearing systems where appropriate:*

    - *cash*

    - *cheques*

    - *plastic cards including credit cards and debit cards*

    - *direct payments, including giro credits and BACS computerised payments*

This chapter lastly describes the policy adopted by the banks for storing documents and electronic data – all of which need to be kept safely and confidentially.

Later chapters in this book go into more detail and describe the internal procedures for checking and validating payments: Chapter 2 'Receiving and recording payments' and Chapter 4 'Making payments'.

BANKS AND BUILDING SOCIETIES IN THE UK

what are banks and building societies?

The banking system in the UK fulfils the important function of accepting deposits and lending money. It basically 'oils the wheels' of the economy. It is made up of a wide variety of banks and a number of building societies.

- a **bank** is a limited company, owned by shareholders; well-known names include Barclays, HSBC, RBS and Lloyds TSB
- a **building society** is a 'mutual' organisation owned by its members (ie its customers); well-known names include Nationwide (the biggest building society) and the smaller Yorkshire Building Society

The trend over the last few decades has been for the banks to 'buy out' building societies by paying the building society members (customers) sizeable sums of money or giving them shares in return for their ownership.

building societies – the services

The services offered by **building societies** are principally to the personal customer market rather than to businesses. These services include:

- deposits: current and savings accounts for the members (customers)
- loans: mortgages for house purchase

Larger building societies also provide property-linked business services. Nationwide, for example, organises finance for property projects, including major housing developments and schools.

banks – the services

Banks have traditionally offered a wide range of services to both personal and business customers. If you work in a finance and accounting role in business you are most likely to be dealing with a bank. The main services they offer to businesses and other organisations include:

- current accounts – dealing with cash, cheques and automated payments
- deposit accounts – paying interest on surplus funds
- overdrafts – flexible borrowing on a current account to cover temporary requirements
- loan accounts – financing loans with flexible repayments
- mortgages – loans for property purchase

These business services are described in more detail on the next page.

banks and building societies – the difference

It is often difficult to tell the difference between banks and building societies in terms of the services they offer. For example Halifax and Santander are both banks whereas Nationwide is a building society. They all look very similar from the 'High Street.' The main difference is the **extra** services offered by the banks, for example:

- **business services**
- **specialised personal services** such as safe custody (looking after the valuables of personal customers), and wills and trusts

Both the banks and the larger building societies offer the same wide range of financial services expected by **personal customers**. These include:

- current accounts, debit and credit cards
- overdrafts, personal loans and mortgages
- insurance, travel money, investments

BANK SERVICES FOR THE BUSINESS CUSTOMER

business current account

A **business current account** is a 'working account' through which day-to-day financial transactions pass, including payments received from customers and payment of business expenses and wages. Payments are made by cheque and also using the BACS (Bankers Automated Clearing Services) computer payment system to send standing orders, direct debits and payments to suppliers. Regular statements are sent by the bank to the business. These will be checked by the business against the bank account in the cash book (see Chapter 5).

A business may arrange for an overdraft on the current account. This means that the business can borrow on a temporary basis from the current account (see the next page).

deposit account

A **deposit account** is used for excess money held by a business, and interest is paid by the bank on the amount deposited. Current account facilities such as cheques, standing orders, direct debits, and overdrafts are not allowed on deposit accounts. Many business customers have both a current and a deposit account. A business can use a deposit account as a temporary 'home' for surplus money, where it can earn interest. When the money is needed it can be transferred on request, or by telephoned or online instructions, to the firm's current account.

Substantial sums of money (normally £500,000 plus) can be placed on deposit with a bank in what are often known as 'treasury accounts'. These accounts may allow withdrawals without notice, or they may need a longer period of notice of withdrawal, perhaps one month or three or six months.

overdraft

An **overdraft** is borrowing from the bank on a current account. If a business considers that it will need an overdraft, it should contact the bank and seek agreement for an overdraft 'facility' up to a certain limit for a specified time. Interest will be charged on overdrawn balances and an arrangement/renewal fee is normally payable. An overdraft is a very flexible arrangement because the customer can borrow when the need arises, and will only pay interest on the amount borrowed.

loan accounts

Whereas an overdraft is a means of borrowing on an ordinary current account and will cover day-to-day expenses of the business, loan accounts are long-term loans for long-term items, eg machinery and new projects. Some typical examples of loan account include:

business loan

A business loan is financing to cover large items of expense such as new machinery, premises expansion or a new project.

- loan amounts can range from £1,000 to £100,000
- interest is paid, either at a rate fixed at the beginning of the loan, or at a variable rate in line with market rates during the lifetime of the loan
- a bank loan is for a set time period, normally between 2 and 30 years
- the loan is often repaid in regular instalments, but this may be varied, for example with a 'repayment holiday' – this is where the borrower is allowed to wait a year or so before starting to make repayments; some loans can also be repaid in full at the end of the loan period

commercial mortgage

A commercial mortgage is a loan for up to twenty-five years to cover the purchase of property (the business equivalent of a 'home loan' mortgage to an individual).

- a mortgage is an arrangement in which property is used as security for borrowing; if the business defaults on the loan, the bank can sell the property to obtain the funds. Amounts range from £25,000 to £500,000
- banks can provide finance for the purchase of commercial property, normally up to 70% of its market value

- interest is paid, either at a rate fixed at the beginning of the mortgage, or at a variable rate in line with market rates during the lifetime of the mortgage

other bank services for businesses

Banks operate a further wide range of services for businesses through their subsidiary companies. If you log onto the websites of HSBC, RBS or Lloyds TSB, you will see example of these, including:

- **debit and credit cards** and card payment processing – issuing company credit cards, processing card payments as a 'card merchant'
- **insurance** – protection for business employees, premises and other risks
- **international services** – currency accounts, overseas payments, dealing with exports and imports

Bank subsidiary companies also help finance businesses through:

- **leasing** – a leasing company buys an asset needed by the business and then 'rents' it out to the business (company cars, for example, are often leased rather than bought outright)
- **factoring** – providing finance to companies against their invoices issued to customers; invoices are effectively 'bought' from the business that issues them and the factoring company then collects the money from the customer when the invoice is due

Bank services to businesses are summarised in the diagram below.

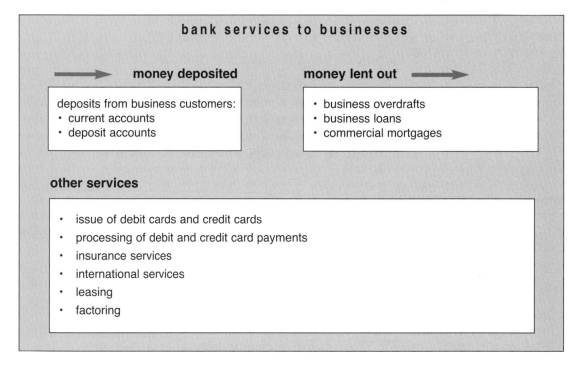

bank services to businesses

money deposited

deposits from business customers:
- current accounts
- deposit accounts

money lent out

- business overdrafts
- business loans
- commercial mortgages

other services

- issue of debit cards and credit cards
- processing of debit and credit card payments
- insurance services
- international services
- leasing
- factoring

The remainder of this chapter explains how the various methods of payment work in practice and how they are 'cleared' – ie processed – through the banking system. Later chapters in this book deal with the ways in which payments received by a business and payments made by a business are checked and validated (where appropriate) and security procedures are followed: see Chapter 2 and Chapter 4.

CASH

Some businesses, shops for example, take cash – notes and coins – in payment for goods and services. They do not, however, use cash as a means of transferring money through the banking system as it is obviously too bulky, a security risk and impractical.

Cash is still one of the simplest methods of making payment for goods and services, particularly where small amounts are involved. However, the suggestion that the 'cashless society' is growing has recently been given support with the introduction of the 'tap and go' card: this is a plastic debit card which is used to make purchases of under £10 just by 'tapping' a retailer terminal and debiting the customer's bank account (see page 12).

The areas where the banks can help businesses with cash include:

- cash paid into their accounts over the counter with a paying-in slip (see below)
- they provide cash when a business needs to pay cash wages
- the night safe facility allows a business to lodge cash in a special wallet which is placed in a special secure 'letter box' in the wall of the bank outside normal banking hours

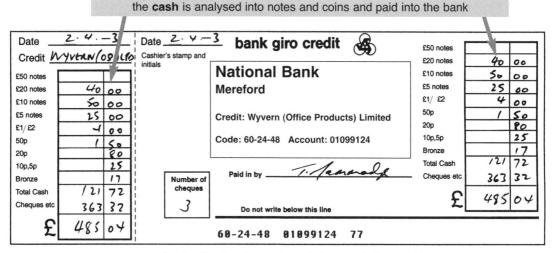

the **cash** is analysed into notes and coins and paid into the bank

a paying in slip showing cash and cheques being paid in

CHEQUES

Cheques are issued by banks and building societies to their current account customers. Payment by cheque is a common method of payment for businesses but is in decline with personal customers – in fact, some large retail stores now refuse to take them, and there are plans to phase them out by 2018. They are still popular, however, for payments made by post, eg payment of bills and payment by business customers who have bought goods and services on credit from businesses. A specimen cheque is shown at the bottom of this page.

what is a cheque?

A cheque is an order in writing and signed by the customer (the 'drawer') telling a bank to pay an amount to someone (the 'payee').

Although some organisations now print out their cheques on computer systems, a large number of cheques used in business are still written by hand. Great care must be taken both when writing out cheques and also when receiving written cheques in payment; they must be checked and examined to ensure that all the details and signatures are correct. If they are not correct in this way they may be invalid.

Note the use of the terms 'payee' and 'drawer' on the cheque shown below.

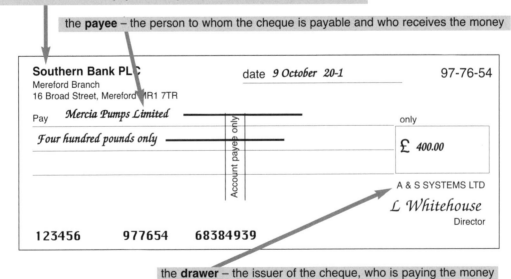

the **bank** that has to pay the cheque out of the issuer's bank account

the **payee** – the person to whom the cheque is payable and who receives the money

the **drawer** – the issuer of the cheque, who is paying the money

the 'parties' to a cheque – the people involved

CHEQUE CLEARING

Every working day cheques are paid into banks and building societies. These cheques are then passed on to the banks of the people and organisations that issued them so that the cheques can be authorised for payment. This process is known as the 'cheque clearing' and a cheque which has been authorised and paid is said to have 'cleared'. Note that cheques paid into building societies are also passed on through this bank clearing system. In other words, **all cheques** pass through the bank clearing system.

If authorisation is not given by the issuer's bank, usually because the issuer of the cheque has not got the money on the account, the cheque will 'bounce' and will be sent back to the bank where it was paid in and the money will be deducted from the account. This is known as a 'dishonoured' cheque.

The problem with this old-fashioned and cumbersome system is that a customer paying in a cheque may not know:

- when the cheque might start to earn interest (if the account pays interest)
- when they can draw out the money that they have paid in
- whether or not the cheque has 'bounced'(returned) – in which case the money will not be available

The '2-4-6' clearance cycle was introduced to sort out these uncertainties.

the 2-4-6 clearance cycle

The numbers in the '2-4-6' clearance cycle refer to the number of working days after paying in a cheque that:

- interest may be paid on the amount paid in (if it is an account that pays interest)
- customers can withdraw the amount paid in
- customers can be absolutely certain that the money is safe in their account and the cheque will not be 'bounced' (returned) and the money taken out again

The actual number of days in each case is calculated as shown below.

Note that 'days' means working days – ie excluding Saturdays, Sundays and bank holidays.

- after **2** working days interest may be paid on the amount paid in

- after **4** working days the amount can be withdrawn from the account

- after **6** working days the money paid in is guaranteed safe and cannot be taken out of the account if the cheque has bounced

There is sometimes confusion about how these 'working days' tie up with the day on which the cheque was paid in. The answer is that the day on which the cheque was paid in **is not counted** as one of the working days.

This can be illustrated using a specific example:

- Ben banks at RBS (Nottingham branch). On **Monday** he pays into the RBS branch a £500 Barclays (Liverpool branch) cheque issued by Tom.

  The cheque is sent off in the cheque clearing by RBS to Barclays (Liverpool) on **Monday**.

- Ben can expect interest to be paid on this £500 (if the account pays interest) **2** working days later, ie on **Wednesday** (Monday + 2 days).

- Ben can withdraw this £500 from the account **4** working days later, ie on **Friday** (Monday + 4 days) but still runs the risk of the cheque being bounced and losing his money.

- Ben can withdraw this £500 from the account **6** working days later, ie by the end of **the following Tuesday** (Monday + 6 working days) and know that the cheque will not bounce and the money cannot be taken off his account.

Now study this process in the diagram below.

the 2-4-6 clearance cycle		
actual day	**working day number**	**stage in the clearance cycle**
Monday	0	the cheque for £500 is paid in and sent off for clearing
Tuesday	1	
Wednesday	2	interest on the £500 may be paid on the account
Thursday	3	
Friday	4	the £500 can be withdrawn, but at the risk of the cheque bouncing and the money being deducted from the account
Saturday Sunday	*It's the weekend – not counted as working days*	
Monday	5	
Tuesday	6	at the end of this day the £500 will be safe and the cheque cannot bounce

PAYMENT BY PLASTIC CARD

There are a number of types of plastic card commonly used as a means of payment. These include:

- **debit cards** - where payment is taken straight from the bank account of the customer
- **prepayment cards** - where a customer has already 'topped up' (prepaid) the card up to a certain value and payment is taken from that value
- **credit cards** - where payment is made by the customer to the credit card issuer at a later date

The normal electronic method used to process the payments for these cards is 'Chip and PIN' technology where the customer is present and enters a PIN (Personal Identification Number) on a terminal, or a remote terminal where the transaction is mail order or online.

DEBIT CARDS

Debit cards are issued to personal customers by banks and building societies to enable their customers to make payments from their bank accounts electronically when they make purchases. No cheque is written out.

Debit cards are issued to selected customers of the bank; they enable a payment to be made from the person's bank account electronically. A debit card has the obvious advantages of being quicker to use and more convenient. Common debit cards issuers include Visa, Maestro and Mastercard. It normally takes up to two days for the amount of a purchase to be taken from the account.

Debit cards often combine a number of functions, which some years ago used to be carried out by separate bank cards. These functions include:

- **debit payment cards** – enabling customers to make payment without having to issue a cheque
- **cash cards** - enabling customers to take cash from cash machines in the UK and foreign currency from cash machines abroad
- **cheque guarantee cards** - used in conjunction with a cheque up to a certain amount, usually £100 or (more commonly) £250, and guaranteeing payment of that cheque

The first two functions listed here – payment transaction and cash withdrawal – are very common but the cheque guarantee function is now rarely used and is due to be phased out shortly because cheques are now not often used to make purchases.

When a customer wishes to pay by debit card in person, eg at a shop, the transaction is processed using an electronic terminal and verified by 'Chip and PIN'. Radio technology has also made possible the **'Tap and Go'** debit cards, for example the Mastercard PayPass, where a simple tap on the terminal at the checkout (in shops and public transport) makes it possible to pay for items under £10 and take the money from the buyer's current account.

PREPAYMENT CARDS

Prepayment cards are becoming increasingly popular. They have the same appearance as debit or credit cards, but there is a major difference: they are purchased by the customer and have a preloaded 'balance to spend' which can be topped up at a bank, Post Office or PayPoint terminal. They can be used for making high street or online purchases, and withdrawing cash – but only up to the limit on the card. They are 'credit cards without the credit.'

They are useful for customers who may have a poor credit rating, or for people under 18, as they can be used internationally. For businesses taking payment they are dealt with in the same way as a debit or credit card.

There is no clearing cycle for these because payment is made in advance.

CREDIT CARDS

Credit cards provide a means of obtaining goods and services immediately, but paying for them later. The most common credit cards used in the UK are issued by Visa and Mastercard.

Credit cards are issued, upon application, to customers of banks, building societies, retail chains and an increasingly wide variety of businesses and other organisations. Goods and services can be obtained at shops and other outlets having computer terminals. Credit cards can also be used for mail order, telephoned and internet sales. Retailers use a **card merchant** to process all their card payments, and pay a set percentage (up to 5%) of each transaction amount for the use of the credit card facility. Each month the cardholder is sent a statement of the purchases made in the previous month and can choose to pay off by a set monthly date the full balance of the account, or to pay part only (subject to a certain minimum amount), carrying forward the remaining balance to the next month. Interest is charged on any balance still owing to the credit card company after the monthly payment date (eg if the minimum amount has been paid). An annual flat fee may be charged to the cardholder for the use of the card.

DIRECT PAYMENTS - BANK GIRO CREDIT

We have already seen earlier in this chapter how money can be paid into a bank account by means of a bank paying-in slip. The banking system also allows for a **bank giro credit** to be paid in at one branch and processed through a **three day clearing system** to another bank or branch. The bank credit clearing system is widely used for paying bills (eg electricity, gas, telephone) and settling credit card accounts.

The preprinted bank giro credit is usually a tear-off slip at the bottom of a bill. The person or business paying the bill will fill in:

- the amount of the payment
- the date that the payment is being made at the bank
- in some cases the signature of the person paying in the credit at the bank

The bill is then taken to the bank and paid in, together with a cheque for the appropriate amount. A water bill is shown below, together with the cheque.

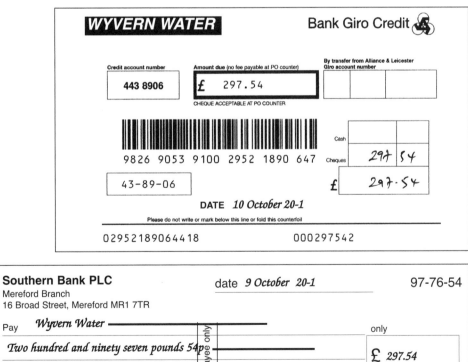

DIRECT PAYMENTS – USING THE BACS

Bankers Automated Clearing Services (BACS) is a computer transfer payment system owned by the banks. It is widely used for regular payments such as insurance premiums, settlement of trade debts, wages and salaries. BACS is a cheap and efficient means of payment because, instead of a piece of paper having to be prepared and despatched, the transfer is set up on a computer file and transferred between the banks' computers – the payment goes direct from account to account.

BACS direct credits

Businesses often need to make regular payments of **variable** amounts, eg:

• paying wages on pay day

• making payments to established suppliers at the end of each month

The banks have established a BACS **direct credit** system to process these variable payments. Whenever the payments are due to be paid the business sends the bank a schedule (faxed or sent electronically) setting out the details of the payments. **The payment cycle is three working days.** If a business wants its suppliers or employees to have the money in their accounts on Friday, the money must leave the business's account on Wednesday. The payment instructions will need to be received by the middle of Wednesday afternoon.

standing orders

The business that needs to make regular payments of the same amount, eg a loan repayment, completes a written authority instructing the bank what payments to make, to whom, and when. The bank then sets up the instructions on its computer, and the payments are made automatically by computer link – using BACS – on the due dates. **Again, the payment cycle is three working days.**

BACS direct debits

The direct debit system is useful for organisations such as insurance companies that receive a large number of variable payments:

• direct debits can be used for either fixed and variable amounts and/or where the time intervals between payments vary

• it is the business that receives payment that prepares the computer instructions requesting the payer's bank account for payment through the banking system; a direct debit is like a standing order or direct credit operating backwards

OTHER 'ONE-OFF' PAYMENTS

In addition to the regular payments processed by BACS standing orders and direct debits, businesses can make 'one-off' payments using the bank computer systems; these include the CHAPS system and the Faster Payments Service. Bank drafts are also widely used for large amount secure payments.

CHAPS

CHAPS (Clearing House Automated Payments System) is used for high value same-day payments sent by the banks through their computer networks. The payment may be in sterling or in euros. CHAPS is used extensively by solicitors when they are arranging the purchase and sale of property for clients. CHAPS payments cannot be cancelled after they have been sent.

Faster Payments Service

In 2008 the main banks and building societies launched the **Faster Payments Service**, the aim of which is to enable customers to send same-day payments from their account to another account at a bank or building society which participates in the scheme. Features of the service include:

- customer instructions for payment may be given at the bank branch, by telephone or over the internet
- customer instructions include the name of the account to receive the payment, the account number, the sort code and any identifying reference number
- the customer must have enough money in the account for the payment
- the payment will normally take only two hours to reach its destination account; once the payment has been sent it cannot be cancelled
- the bank sending the payment will receive an acknowledgement that the payment has been made when it reaches its destination account; if there is a problem with the payment at the receiving bank it will be rejected and the sending bank will be notified

The **Faster Payments Service** is intended for smaller and medium-sized amounts. Larger amounts are normally sent by CHAPS.

bank drafts

An organisation may have to make a large purchase – for example new vehicles – and be asked to pay by bank draft. A bank draft is a cheque written out by a bank. It is a guaranteed means of payment which is as good as cash, but without the security risks that cash involves.

BANK POLICY – RETENTION OF DOCUMENTS

filing retention policy

Over the years banks are likely to accumulate a large volume of paper-based documents, for example:

- customer correspondence and printouts
- paid cheques
- standing order and direct debit payment authorities
- debit and cheque card agreement forms

Banks, like all businesses, should have a **retention policy** stating that records are normally kept for **six years, plus the current year**.

The reasons for this are legal requirements. Legislation covering company law, taxation and data protection generally requires that records should be kept for anywhere between three and six years.

Another legal reason is that **after six years** if anyone wants to take a legal action against a business, they are prevented from doing so by a principle known as **limitation of action**. That is why all necessary evidence is kept for at least six years.

safe keeping and security documents

Banks have to deal with valuable documents for two main reasons:

- **safe keeping** (safe custody) – shares and investment certificates and other valuables kept locked in the safe for customers, often in deed boxes – these are obviously held as long as the customer wants them kept there
- **security documents** – a business customer may borrow money and be asked to deposit property deeds or sign a guarantee to cover that borrowing – these security documents should be kept for legal reasons by the bank for **twelve** years after the borrowing has been repaid

destruction of filing records

Any business should always keep its records secure and so that nobody who is not authorised to access the records can get hold of confidential information. This is particularly important for banks because if fraudsters get hold of customer names and bank account numbers, they can also get hold of money from customers' accounts. After the six years has elapsed these records should be destroyed or shredded (paper records), or 'wiped' (data held electronically). This includes the wiping or destruction of a computer's hard disk if a computer is being replaced.

Chapter Summary

■ The UK banking system is made up of **banks** and **building societies**; banks are limited companies whereas building societies are mutual organisations owned by their members.

■ **Building societies** offer services predominantly to personal customers (deposits and mortgages) whereas the **banks** offer services to both personal and business customers.

■ The main services offered by the banks to **business customers** include: current accounts, deposit accounts, overdrafts, loan accounts and commercial mortgages. Other services for business customers include card issue and payments processing, insurance, international services, leasing and factoring.

■ **Forms of payment** which operate within the banking system include cash, cheque, debit cards, prepayment cards, credit cards and direct payments such as giro credits and BACS payments.

■ **Cash** is one of the simplest and best forms of payment for small value transactions.

■ **Cheques** are still commonly used for postal payments, to which they are ideally suited. Cheques are subject to the '2-4-6' clearance cycle which means that following the paying in day:

 - interest can be paid on the cheque amount paid in 2 working days later

 - the cheque amount can be withdrawn 4 working days later

 - the cheque cannot be returned unpaid 6 working days later

■ **Debit cards** are commonly used for purchases. The amount of the purchase is normally taken from the bank account within two days.

■ **Credit cards** can be used to make purchases and payment will be made about a month later on the receipt of a statement.

■ **Bank giro credits** are a paper-based direct payment system for paying bills and making other payments through the banking system. Clearance time is three days.

■ The computer-based **BACS system** is used for making direct payments by standing order, direct debit and direct credit. The clearance cycle is three days.

■ The **Faster Payments Service** is a same-day two hour computer payment service used by the banks for telephoned and online payments and **CHAPS** is a same-day high-value computer payment service.

■ Banks maintain a strict **document retention policy**, which for most documents is a period of at least six years.

Key
Terms

current account	an account which is used for day-to-day payments
deposit account	an account which pays interest and is used for savings and surplus money
overdraft	a current account from which a customer may borrow from time to time
business loan	a long-term loan with an agreed repayment programme, used for financing a business
commercial mortgage	a long-term loan to finance the purchase of property
cheque	a written instruction to a bank by a customer (the drawer) to pay a specified amount of money to a specified person (the payee) – clearance using the 2-4-6 day cycle (see Chapter Summary)
debit card	a card issued to a customer which can be used for purchases and cash withdrawals; payment is taken from the account within two days
credit card	a card issued to a customer on a 'buy now and pay later' basis; payment is made on receipt of a statement
prepayment card	a card which can be purchased and given a 'balance to spend' – useful when the customer is under 18
bank giro credit	a paper-based direct payment through the banking system with a three day clearance cycle
BACS	Bankers Automated Clearing Services - a three day computer-based direct payment system
BACS direct credit	direct BACS payments – with a three day clearance
standing order	regular BACS payments, set up with the bank by the customer paying the amounts
direct debit	regular and variable BACS payments, set up by the organisation receiving the payments
Faster Payments Service	same day payments (usually 2 hours) between banks and building societies – instructions normally given by telephone or online
CHAPS	high value, same day, payments sent through the banks' computer systems
bank draft	a cheque written out by a bank – as good as cash – used for high value purchases

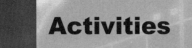

Activities

1.1 A building society is set up as:

(a) a public limited company owned by shareholders

(b) a mutual organisation owned by its customers

Which one of these options is correct?

1.2 Building societies offer a full range of business services to their customers.
True or false?

1.3 An overdraft:

(a) is only available to business customers

(b) is only available to personal customers

(c) is available to both business and personal customers

(d) is repayable in fixed instalments

(e) is charged a fixed amount of interest each month

(f) is only charged interest on the amounts borrowed each month

Which two of these options are correct?

1.4 A cheque is:

(a) an instruction to a customer to pay to the bank a specific amount of money

(b) an instruction to a bank to pay to a specified person a specific amount of money

(c) an instruction to a specified person to pay a specific amount of money

Which one of these options is correct?

1.5 The bank cheque clearing is called the 2-4-6 system because the numbers relate to the number of working days after the cheque is cleared that:

(a) the customer can withdraw the money amount of the cheque

(b) the cheque is guaranteed not to be returned ('bounced')

(c) interest can be paid (if applicable) on the amount of the cheque paid in

You are to state which of the three numbers (2-4-6) applies to statements (a), (b) and (c).

1.6 A 'Chip and PIN' debit card can be used to make a purchase through a shop terminal even if there is not enough money available in the account of the cardholder.

True or false?

1.7 A credit card allows payment:

(a)   of the full amount by the given date and no interest will be payable

(b)   of the minimum amount by the given date and no interest will be payable

(c)   whenever the cardholder wants and interest will be payable straightaway

Which one of these options is correct?

1.8 A bank giro credit is:

(a)   an online direct payment which is used to pay variable amounts owing

(b)   a paper-based direct payment which is used to pay variable amounts owing

(c)   a computer-based direct payment which is used to pay variable amounts owing

Which one of these options is correct?

1.9 Which plastic card requires the card holder to pay for purchase transactions in advance?

(a)   a credit card

(b)   a debit card

(c)   a prepayment card

Which one of these options is correct?

1.10 BACS standing orders are best suited for payments which:

(a)   are equal in amount

(b)   are variable in amount

(c)   are made on different dates in the month

Which one of these options is correct?

1.11 CHAPS stands for:

(a)   Cheque Handling Automated Payments System

(b)   Clearing House Automated Payments System

(c)   Clearing House Advanced Payment System

Which one of these options is correct?

1.12 The Faster Payments Service normally makes payment to the account in:

(a)   two minutes

(b)   two hours

(c)   two days

Which one of these options is correct?

1.13 The document retention policy of a bank is normally for a period of:

(a)   six months

(b)   six years

(c)   ten years

Which one of these options is correct?

1.14 You are running a business and need to make various payments each month. Which method of payment from the list provided at the end of the question would you choose as the best to use in the following situations:

(a)   paying variable amounts to twenty suppliers at the end of each month

(b)   paying a monthly rates bill of twelve fixed instalments of £258.90

(c)   buying a new car costing £34,000 for the finance director

(d)   settling an electricity bill which has variable quarterly payments

(e)   buying a jar of coffee for office use from the local foodstore

(f)   paying £350,000 to a firm of solicitors for the purchase of a new shop

List of possible means of payment:

1   standing order

2   cash which you can claim back from the person who operates the petty cash

3   bank draft

4   direct debit

5   CHAPS payment

6   BACS direct credit

2 Receiving and recording payments

this chapter covers...

The last chapter described in outline the different ways of paying using the banking system. This chapter concentrates on the practicalities of the payments system. It explains the different ways in which money paid by customers is received by a business:

- cash

- cheques

- BACS transfers

In each case it describes the checks that should be made and the security procedures carried out to ensure that:

- the right amount is received

- from the right person

- and that the payment is properly authorised and will not be refused by the bank

This chapter sets out the procedures that should be followed by the business in documenting and recording those payments, for example:

- checking the cash and issuing receipts

- checking the cheques received

- receiving and processing incoming payments by debit card and credit card

- recording incoming payments on remittance lists, cash books and cash tills

The next chapter explains how money is paid into the bank and is then recorded by the bank on the bank statement.

INCOMING PAYMENTS

Payments can be received by a business in a variety of ways:

- cash (ie banknotes and coins)
- cheques
- credit card and debit card transactions (which can be manually or electronically processed)
- direct to the bank by inter-bank transfer: BACS and CHAPS

The current trend is for more and more payments to be made electronically rather than by cheque, although low value payments are still frequently made by cash.

CASH

Cash, as noted above, is commonly used for most low value transactions, and we still have not reached the 'cashless society' which is sometimes talked about. Eventually, devices such as '**tap and go**' debit cards, which do not require entry of a PIN number, will be widely used for small purchases.

Nowadays, however, as far as the business accepting payments in cash is concerned, the main disadvantage of cash is the security problem, and the risk of receiving forged notes.

receiving payment in cash

For a business receiving sums of money in the form of cash it is necessary for an employee to count the cash received and check it against the amount handed over.

Change will need to be given when the exact amount is not paid. For example if someone buys a magazine for £3.99 and hands over a £10 note:

Sale of magazine	£3.99
Amount given by customer	£10.00
Change to be given by shop	£6.01

The amount of change is the difference between the amount handed over and the amount of the sale. A till will normally indicate the amount of change to be given after the amount handed over has been entered through the keypad.

Often when payment is made in cash, a receipt is given: this can take the form of a till receipt, such as is given in a shop, or a handwritten receipt. Look at these two examples of receipts:

Everest Sports	◄—————	retailer
15 High St Mereford	◄—————	address
08 10 20-3 15.07	◄—————	date and time of transaction
Salesperson Tina	◄—————	salesperson
Tennis balls 5.99	◄—————	goods purchased
Shin guards 18.99	◄—————	goods purchased
TOTAL 24.98	◄—————	total due
CASH 40.00	◄—————	£40 (probably two £20 notes) given by the customer
CHANGE 15.02	◄—————	change given
Thank you for your custom	◄—————	personal message to help public relations
Please retain this receipt in case of any query	◄—————	advice to retain receipt in case of a problem with the goods
VAT REG 373 2888 11	◄—————	VAT Registration number of retailer

a till receipt

ENIGMA MUSIC LIMITED   *receipt*   958

13 High Street, Mereford MR1 2TF
VAT Reg 343 7645 23

Customer .... *R V Williams* ....date ... *3 Oct 20-3* ....

'Golden Oldies' by J Moore	£20.00
	£20.00
VAT @ 17.5%	£3.50
Total	£23.50

a hand-written receipt

tills and cash floats

At the end of the day it is necessary to 'cash up' by totalling the cash held and then agreeing that total with the amount that the till started with at the beginning of the day, plus what has been received during the day. Most cash tills start each day with a float of cash and so the amount in the till at the end of the day should be:

> cash float at start
>
> *plus* sales made during the day (listed on the till roll)
>
> *equals* amount of cash held at end of day

A cash float will be kept back for the following day, and any surplus will be transferred to the safe for paying into the bank next day.

guidelines for cash handling

Cash is often a target for theft – and regrettably not only from people outside the business. General security guidelines for looking after cash received will vary according to the size and type of business:

- cash should be kept in a cash till or in a cash box which should be kept locked when not in use
- the keys should be retained under the control of the cashier
- as little cash as is practically possible should be kept in tills
- cash should be paid into the bank as soon as possible

'topping up' the petty cash

The business may also operate a petty cash system for making small payments (see Chapter 7). The cash will be kept in a locked metal box and will need to be 'topped up' from time-to-time to what is known as the **imprest amount** to bring it up to a fixed level. The principle is basically the same as filling up a car with fuel – you put in the same amount as you have used. Care will have to be taken when transferring money from the main cash fund to the petty cash box: security precautions should be observed.

ACCEPTING CHEQUES

Businesses receive cheques as a form of payment in a variety of ways, either through the post with a remittance advice, or directly over the counter, as in the case of a shop.

Before a cheque is paid into the bank it is very important that it is checked to make sure that it is technically correct.

If you are receiving payment by cheque, whether it is direct from the customer over the counter or through the post on a remittance advice, there are a number of basic checks to carry out:

- is the cheque signed? – it is invalid if it is not
- is the payee's name correct? – it should be changed and initialled by the drawer (person writing out the cheque) if it is not
- is the cheque in date? – a cheque becomes out of date ('stale') and invalid after six months; note that if the date is missing, it may be written in
- do the words and figures agree? – the cheque may be returned by the bank if they do not

Now study the cheque on the next page. The cheque was received by the payee on 20 October 2010. Is it technically correct?

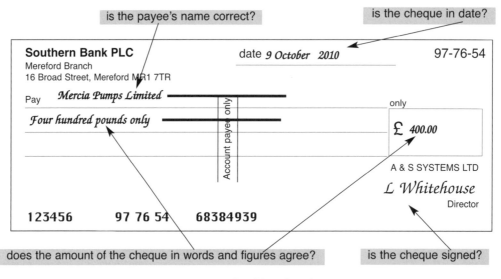

checking the cheque

The answer to 'is this cheque correct' is 'yes' – as long as the payee's name is 'Mercia Pumps Limited.'

But if the business accepting payment by cheque is inefficient and does not carry out the checks listed on the previous page, the cheque concerned may be returned to the business's bank after it has been paid in, and the amount of the cheque deducted from the business's bank account. This is known as a **dishonoured cheque**.

DISHONOURED CHEQUES

returned cheques

A business may be in the unfortunate position of having paid in a cheque and then discovering that the cheque has been returned to its bank **unpaid**, and the amount of the cheque then deducted from the bank account.

The bank will normally post the cheque back to the business that paid it in. If this happens to you when you are working in an Accounts Department and you receive a returned (dishonoured) cheque, you will see that it will have one of a number of reasons for return written or stamped across the top:

- **refer to drawer** – the person or business that has written out the cheque (the issuer or 'drawer') has no money in the bank; this is bad news for you and you will have to contact him or her for an explanation!

   This answer is often abbreviated to 'RD'

- **refer to drawer, please represent** – this means that there was not enough money in the account to meet the cheque, but that the cheque has been sent through the clearing again (represented) in the hope that it will be paid when it reaches the issuers bank the second time (note that in this case the cheque will *not* be sent back to the payee)

  This answer is abbreviated to 'RDPR'

- **payment countermanded by order of drawer** – the cheque has been **stopped** – in other words the issuer (drawer) has told the bank that the cheque should not be paid, maybe because of some dispute or a cancelled order; you should contact the issuer to find out the reason

- **technical problems** – as mentioned before, payment of a cheque may be refused by the bank for technical reasons; you may get a cheque sent back to you with a reason written on the cheque such such as

  – signature required

  – words and figures differ

  – out of date

  This means that you will have to contact the issuer of the cheque (drawer) for a signature (if it is missing), or an alteration (which will have to be signed by the drawer) if the returned cheque is out of date. As you will appreciate, this reinforces the point that a cheque must be carefully checked when it is received in payment.

ACCEPTING CARD PAYMENTS – MODERN METHODS

By far the most common method of processing a debit or credit card payment for a customer who calls in person is **'chip and PIN'** – here the customer authorises payment on a terminal using a four digit number known as a 'PIN' (Personal Identification Number).

terminal 'chip and PIN' sales – customer present

This method of accepting payment by credit and debit cards involves the cardholder's card being inserted in a card reader device with a keypad, eg in a supermarket or a restaurant. The keypad may be wired into a till (as in a supermarket) or it may be mobile and operate through a bluetooth system (as in a restaurant). The customer then confirms the sales transaction (or the bill for the meal) by keying in a four digit number (PIN) which should only be known to the cardholder. If there is any problem (eg the card is stolen or the limit exceeded) authorisation will be refused. This form of payment is good for the seller because it is guaranteed.

The payment itself is processed by a system known as **EFTPOS** (Electronic Funds Transfer at Point of Sale). This sets up through a terminal – at the point of sale – the electronic transfer of the transaction amount from the bank account or credit card account of the purchaser to the seller's bank account.

'Chip and PIN' was introduced for three main reasons:

- it greatly increases the efficiency of checkouts because it saves time
- it cuts down on card fraud because it is a far more secure method of making payment
- it removes the need for telephone calls to be made for authorisation for transactions over the 'floor limit' of the seller (the 'floor limit' is the amount over which a telephone request for authorisation had to be made)

Major benefits of the system are that a chip and PIN transaction avoids the retailer having to carry out all the security checks needed when a signature is required, and the payment is then guaranteed. There are, of course, some common sense precautions which should be taken by the retailer, for example making sure that other customers (or employees) cannot watch or somehow record the PIN being entered.

mail order/telephone sales – customer not present

Buying goods and services by credit card and debit card over the telephone, and by mail order is also very common. Obviously 'chip and PIN' cannot be used for this because the customer is not present. Most businesses will therefore use an electronic **'customer not present'** terminal which will be linked to the card merchant electronically. Note that a very small minority of businesses may still use a mechanical imprinter.

When accepting **'customer not present'** payment by debit or credit card by telephone or mail order, the following details must be obtained:

- the card number, the three digit security code, and expiry date
- the issue number and/or start date of any debit card
- the name and initials of the cardholder as shown on the card
- the cardholder's address
- the cardholder's signature (mail order only)

One important difference for mail order, telephone (and internet) sales is that payment is not necessarily guaranteed. The **chargeback** system means that a purchaser who places an order and then receives faulty or incorrect goods can claim the money back from the card issuing company who refunds it to the purchaser's account. The money is then 'charged back' to the seller. Chargeback can also be used if an unauthorised fraudulent purchase has been made by someone other than the cardholder.

CARD PAYMENTS – OLDER METHODS

'customer present' sales requiring a signature

This older method of using a terminal to process card payments is rapidly being superseded by 'chip and PIN' (see page 27). It may occasionally be used, for example, when the 'chip and PIN' system has broken down. With this 'signature' system the assistant operating the terminal should:

- in the case of a shop till, 'swipe' the card through the card reader – this 'captures' the details encoded in the magnetic stripe on the reverse of the card or in the chip embedded in the card

- the card merchant's system checks automatically that
  - the card number is valid
  - the card has not been lost or stolen
  - there is enough money (or limit) available to pay for the transaction

- if all is well, each transaction will be allowed to pass through; if it is not, the customer will be asked to pay another way

- if the amount is above the 'floor limit', a telephone call to the card merchant will be required to authorise the transaction

- the till prints a two-part receipt which includes space for the cardholder's signature

- the customer signs, and the signature is compared with that on the card

- the customer is handed the top-copy of the receipt, and the other copy is kept in the event of a query in the future

There are a number of **checks** that should be made on the rare occasions when accepting payment authorised by a signature – eg if the 'chip and PIN' system has gone offline and a signature will be needed. These checks apply equally to debit cards and to credit cards.

You should make sure that:

- the card has an appropriate logo, eg 'Maestro' – you will probably have a list against which you can compare the logo

- the card has a magnetic stripe on the reverse or an embedded chip

- the card has not expired

- the start date on the card is not in the future

- the cardholder title is appropriate (eg a card issued to Miss Helen Jones is not used by a man!)

- the signature on the card is consistent and has not been tampered with

- the card has not been defaced or mutilated in any way

- any photograph on the card looks like the customer

mechanical 'push-pull' imprinter machine

This old system is now rarely used, but it is still valid. The procedure is:

- check any photograph on the card and make sure that the card has not been defaced or tampered with
- check that the card has not expired and place it on the imprinter
- imprint the sales voucher by hand on the 'push-pull' mechanical printer
- complete the sales voucher with date, details of goods, and the amount
- the customer signs the imprinted sales voucher, and the signature should be compared with that on the card
- if the payment is above a certain amount – the **floor limit** (which varies according to the type of business) it will be necessary to telephone the card merchant company to obtain an authorisation code for the transaction – the authorisation code is recorded on the sales voucher
- the top copy of the sales voucher is handed to the customer, and the other three copies are retained
- of the three copies of the sales voucher which are retained, the white copy is treated in the same way as a cheque, and is kept in the till and added to the cheques and cash received to give the total sales figure; the other two copies (yellow and blue) are kept in the event of a query in the future
- the white copy of the sales voucher kept in the till is then banked along with the cash and cheques (see next chapter)

floor limits and authorisations (not 'chip and PIN')

When an older system is in use it may be necessary from time-to-time for a business accepting a debit or credit card payment to seek authorisation for the transaction from the card merchant company. Authorisation can be given over the telephone or in some cases electronically when:

- the amount of the transaction exceeds the floor limit – this limit is a transaction amount set by the card merchant company – it can vary
- the terminal indicates that the card is not valid (it may be out of date)
- the cashier is suspicious about the signature
- the cashier is suspicious about the customer
- the terminal indicates that the cashier should contact the card merchant company (it may be a stolen card)

These authorisations are important because if they are not carried out the business accepting payment may lose the money – it will not be a guaranteed payment. **Remember that this authorisation procedure only applies to systems which are not 'chip and PIN' (which automatically removes the need for all these precautions).**

INTERNET PAYMENT TRANSACTIONS

Businesses which have online facilities for selling their products from their websites carry out these sales on a 'remote control' basis. They do not deal with these customers personally. The customers order and pay for the goods on-line using a credit or debit card and all the business has to do is despatch the goods (eg an online shop) or provide the service (eg a holiday company). The money is credited (added) directly to the bank account of the business by the card merchant that processes the payment.

The business will receive from the card merchant a schedule of the payments received which it can check against its bank statement.

The buying public is naturally concerned about the security of buying online. There are many stories of people hacking into shop and bank websites and obtaining names and credit card numbers and then going on spending sprees. Businesses setting up online selling facilities have to ensure that the security of the system is as safe as it can be. Software companies are constantly working to improve levels of security and methods of encoding data ('encryption') so that payment details – including card numbers – remain secret. The padlock symbol on a website means that the data is encrypted.

The mechanics of how the payment from an internet purchase reaches the bank account of the seller is explained in detail on page 48.

CHECKING PAYMENTS AGAINST DOCUMENTATION

It is important that incoming payments received from customers are checked against any documentation that the supplier receives. This is to ensure that the correct amount is received and that no future disputes can arise – for example "We sent you £450, that's what it says on our advice" ... "No you didn't, you only sent us £405, that's what it shows on your account."

The most common type of document which advises the amount of a payment is a **remittance advice**. Payments from customers can be received either through the post, or through the bank as inter-bank transfers. A remittance advice will be issued in both instances by the person paying (see next page).

cheque payments – remittance advice

Any cheque received through the post should be checked for technical irregularities and also against the remittance advice. The business receiving payment must check that the total of the items being paid less any credit due equals the amount of the cheque. Failure to carry out this simple check could cause problems later on if there is a discrepancy. Any discrepancies should be queried with the customer without delay.

inter-bank transfers – BACS remittance advice

An increasing number of payments are now made automatically from bank account to bank account, normally on the instructions of the payer, through the BACS system (BACS stands for Bankers Automated Clearing Services). Because no cheque is issued, payment is made more quickly and more cheaply. With this system the buyer sends to the seller a BACS advice – essentially a remittance advice for a BACS payment. The business receiving payment will have to check each advice carefully against the bank statement when it arrives to ensure that the correct amount has been received. Two remittance advices are shown below – a cheque one and a BACS one.

TO	**REMITTANCE ADVICE**	FROM
Cool Socks Limited Unit 45 Elgar Estate, Broadfield, BR7 4ER	8 November 20-3	**Vogue Ltd** 56 Shaftesbury Road Manorfield MA1 6GP

date	your reference	our reference	payment amount
03 11 -3	INVOICE 788106	876213	500.00
15 11 -3	INVOICE 788256	876287	220.10
20 11 -3	CREDIT NOTE 12218	876287	(22.01)
		CHEQUE TOTAL	698.09

BACS REMITTANCE ADVICE

FROM: Trends
4 Friar Street
Broadfield BR1 3RF

TO
Cool Socks Limited
Unit 45 Elgar Estate, Broadfield, BR7 4ER

06 11 -3

Your ref	Our ref		Amount
787923	47609	BACS TRANSFER	249.57
		TOTAL	249.57

THIS HAS BEEN PAID BY BACS CREDIT TRANSFER DIRECTLY INTO YOUR BANK ACCOUNT AT ALBION BANK NO 11451226 SORT CODE 90 47 17

RECORDING MONEY RECEIVED

The individual amounts of money received should be recorded by the business. The way in which they are recorded will depend on the way in which they are received. The fact that the amounts are recorded will help security by discouraging theft by employees.

cash tills

Money received over a counter is likely to be recorded on a cash till tally roll or electronic till memory – the totals on the till roll or memory can then be checked with the actual money received, ready for paying into the bank. The security of cash tills is tightly controlled: they are operated by a security key and any transfer of change is recorded.

remittance lists (postal items)

Cheques and other money received may be recorded manually on a **remittance list**. 'Remittance list' just means a list of what you have been sent. It can record items received through the post by a business, or it can be used at the counter of old-fashioned shops instead of a cash till. A remittance list for items received through the post is likely to include columns for the date, sender, the nature of the 'remittance' amount, and, as a security measure, the signature of the person opening the post. A remittance list will normally be totalled from time-to-time.

date	sender	remittance	amount	signature
12.3.20-3	Travers Toys Ltd	cheque	234.50	G Palmer
12.3.20-3	Grampian Traders	bank draft	10,500.00	G Palmer
12.3.20-3	Mrs D Dodds	cash	14.50	R Patel
12.3.20-3	Mercia Foods	cheque	450.00	G Palmer

extract from a remittance list for items received through the post

cash book – a book of prime entry

The cash book is the book of prime entry for money amounts received and paid out by the organisation in the form of cash and as items passed through the bank account. All the receipts referred to in this chapter will eventually pass through the cash book. It will be dealt with in detail in Chapter 5.

■ **Incoming payments** can be received in a number of ways: cash, cheque, credit and debit card, inter-bank transfer from BACS and internet sales.

■ **Receipts** are often issued for cash payments; either till receipts or handwritten receipts.

■ **Cash** in a till will be counted up at the end of each day; the amount should equal the takings for the day plus any 'float' held in the till.

■ **Cheques** should be examined carefully when received as payment, details to be checked include the signature, payee's name, the date and the amount in words and figures.

■ Cheques returned by the bank unpaid are known as **dishonoured cheques** – this can happen if the cheque has technical errors, or is stopped, or if the person or business issuing it does not have the money in the bank.

■ **Debit cards** are commonly accepted as a means of payment in place of cash or cheques. They are normally processed using a 'chip and PIN' electronic terminal.

■ Payment can also be accepted by **credit card** – normally using a 'chip and PIN' electronic terminal.

■ If a business uses a 'chip and PIN' electronic terminal or remote 'customer not present' terminal the money will be transferred electronically from the customer's bank account or credit card account to the business bank account. This system is known as **EFTPOS** (Electronic Funds Transfer at Point Of Sale).

■ Older methods of processing credit and debit card payments include the '**customer signature**' system and also the antiquated '**imprinter**' machine. These methods are rapidly dying out.

■ Sales transactions over the **Internet** are processed under secure conditions and the money transferred automatically to the seller's bank account.

■ When payments are accompanied by documentation such as a **remittance advice**, the payment should be checked against the documentation. Payment in this case is likely to be by cheque or by inter-bank transfer.

■ When money is received it should be **recorded**, both for security purposes and also as part of the operation of the accounting system. Forms of recording include the cash till roll, remittance lists and the cash book.

Key Terms

cash float	the amount of cash kept in a till at the end of the day to provide change when the till is next used
drawer of a cheque	the person who signs the bottom of the cheque – the customer from whose account the money is to be paid
payee of a cheque	the person to whom the cheque is payable – normally specified on the first line of the cheque after the word 'pay'
dishonoured cheque	a cheque which is paid in but then returned unpaid to the payee because of a technical error or because the drawer does not have the money
debit card	a plastic card which enables customers to make payment for purchases without having to write out a cheque – payment is made electronically from the bank account
credit card	a plastic card issued by a credit card company which enables customers to make purchases and pay for them at a later date
chip and PIN	the technology for accepting payments by debit and credit cards where the customer enters a four digit number (PIN) into an electronic terminal
EFTPOS	Electronic Funds Transfer at Point Of Sale – the electronic transfer of payments between the accounts of buyer and seller originated at the point of sale, eg a shop till
BACS	BACS stands for Bankers Automated Clearing Services, a body (owned by the banks) which organises computer payments between bank accounts
remittance advice	a document sent to the recipient of a payment, advising that a payment is being made
remittance list	a record of money amounts received by a business

Activities

2.1 You operate the cash till at the firm where you work. The following are the sales for one day:

		Amount of sale £	Notes and/or coin tendered
Customer	1	8.50	£10 note
	2	3.30	£10 note
	3	2.51	£5 note
	4	1.79	£5 note
	5	0.34	£1 coin
	6	6.22	£10 note
	7	12.76	£20 note
	8	1.42	two £1 coins
	9	6.54	£10 note
	10	3.08	£5 note

Calculate:
(a) the amount of change to be given to each customer
(b) the notes and/or coins that will be given in change, using the minimum number possible

2.2 If the cash till in Activity 2.1 had a float of £28.71 at the start of the day, how much cash should be held in the till after the sales from activity 1 had been made? Present your answer in the following form:

	£
cash float at start	28.71
plus sales made during the day	_____
equals amount of cash held at end of day	══════

2.3 You work as a shop counter assistant at New Era Lighting. You make a number of sales during the day (use today's date) which require the completion of a handwritten receipt. Complete the receipts set out on the next page. Include VAT on all purchases at 17.5%. All prices quoted here are catalogue prices and exclude VAT.

(a) 2 flexilamps @ £13.99, 2 60w light bulbs @ 85p, to Mr George Ohm

NEW ERA LIGHTING   977

17 High Street, Mereford, MR1 2TF
VAT Reg 141 7654 23

CASH RECEIPT

Customer ....date.................

VAT	
TOTAL	

(b) 1 standard lamp @ £149.95, 1 13amp plug @ 99p, to Mr Alex Bell

NEW ERA LIGHTING   978

17 High Street, Mereford, MR1 2TF
VAT Reg 141 7654 23

CASH RECEIPT

Customer ....date.................

VAT	
TOTAL	

(c) 2 external Georgian lamps @ £35.99, to Tom Edison

NEW ERA LIGHTING   979

17 High Street, Mereford, MR1 2TF
VAT Reg 141 7654 23

CASH RECEIPT

Customer ....date.................

VAT	
TOTAL	

2.4 You work as an accounts assistant at Electron Games Limited. You have received the three cheques shown below though the post in settlement of customer accounts. Check them carefully and state what is wrong with them. Assume that the date today is 12 October 2013.

(a)

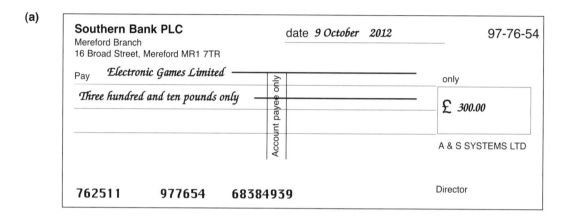

Southern Bank PLC
Mereford Branch
16 Broad Street, Mereford MR1 7TR

date *9 October 2012*   97-76-54

Pay   *Electronic Games Limited*   only

Three hundred and ten pounds only

Account payee only

£ *300.00*

A & S SYSTEMS LTD

762511   977654   68384939   Director

(b)

Western Bank PLC
Barfield Branch
3, The Square, Barfield BR1 2GH

date *6 October 2013*   66-01-29

Pay   *Electron Games Limited*   only

Two hundred and ninety five pounds only

Account payee only

£ *295.10*

N G HAPLISS

N G Hapliss

652109   660129   16349531

(c)

Northern Bank PLC
Instone Branch
45 High Street, Instone IN3 2BD

date *3 February 2013*   87-76-22

Pay   *Electron Games Limited*   only

Forty nine pounds 79p

Account payee only

£ *47.99*

B GUNN LTD

B Gunn

185346   877622   86431906   Director

2.5   If a cheque is returned to the business which has paid it in marked 'refer to drawer' it means that:

(a)   there is a technical problem with the cheque, for example it could be out of date

(b)   the issuer's signature is missing and will have to be obtained as soon as possible

(c)   the issuer of the cheque does not have enough money in the account to pay the cheque

(d)   the cashier must check the list of stolen cheques kept in the till drawer

Which one of these options is correct?

2.6   If a debit or credit card is used for making payment at a supermarket till using 'chip and PIN' the customer should:

(a)   enter the PIN number on the card reader and sign a voucher to authorise the payment

(b)   enter the PIN number on the card reader and tell the cashier the security number on the back of the card

(c)   enter the PIN number on the card reader and tell the cashier the PIN number to confirm the transaction

(d)   enter the PIN number on the card reader, making sure that no-one has seen them keying in the numbers

Which one of these options is correct?

2.7   When a mail order company accepts debit and credit card payments from customers who order goods through the post:

(a)   the payment to the seller will be guaranteed in all circumstances

(b)   the payment may not be guaranteed and may be refunded to the customer through 'chargeback'

(c)   the PIN number will need to be input on the mail order company's terminal

(d)   the PIN number and the three digit security code will need to be input on the terminal

Which one of these options is correct?

2.8   EFTPOS stands for:

(a)   Electronic Funds Transfer at Point of Sale

(b)   Express Funds Transit at Point of Sale

(c)   Express Financial Transaction for Purchases and Sales

(d)   Electronic Funds Transaction for Purchases and Sales

Which one of these options is correct?

2.9   What is the purpose of 'encryption' of credit and debit card data in online payment processing? How can you tell from a website that data will be encrypted?

2.10   What is the difference between a remittance advice and a remittance list?

3 Paying into the bank

this chapter covers...

The last chapter dealt with the day-to-day detail of a business receiving payments in the form of cash, cheques, and debit and credit card transactions. It described the checks and precautions that have to be made to ensure that each transaction is secure and accurately recorded.

This chapter deals with the next step in the process and sets out the procedures for paying money into the bank and tracking incoming receipts made electronically.

Before reading this chapter you should be familiar with the contents of Chapter 1 'Introduction to Banking Procedures' (pages 2-21) which provides essential background information for dealing with banks and banking transactions.

This chapter specifically covers the areas of:

- *how to prepare a paying-in slip for paying cash and cheques into the bank*

- *checking the cash and cheques being paid in*

- *preparing the credit card vouchers summary for paying in at the bank*

- *paying in procedures*

- *the need to pay in promptly and security procedures for looking after money*

- *automated payments into the bank account, online payments received and the need for security of electronic data*

- *the format and content of a bank statement*

- *checking the transactions on a bank statement*

PAYING-IN SLIPS

Business customers are issued with a **paying-in book** by the bank. These books are pre-printed and encoded with the customer's name and account number together with details of the bank branch. The details to be completed before paying in at the bank are:

- a summary of the different categories of notes or coins being paid in, the amount of each category being entered on the slip

- amounts and details of cheques being paid in, usually entered on the reverse of the slip, with the total entered on the front

- the cash and cheques being paid in are totalled to give the amount being paid in

- the counterfoil (the section on the left-hand side) is completed

- the person paying in will sign the slip

A completed paying-in slip (both front and back) is illustrated below:

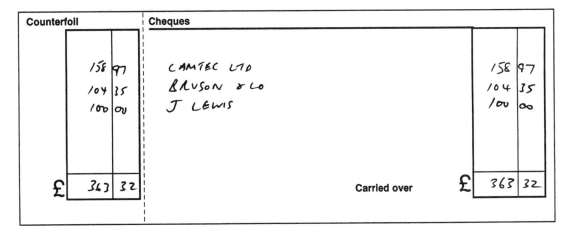

PROCEDURES FOR PAYING IN

the accounting process

Cash and cheques paid in at the bank will normally have been received by the business both as cash sales and also on remittance advices from customers, and so form part of the accounting process. We will see how they are entered in the cash book in Chapter 5.

preparing the cash

Bank notes should be counted, checked and sorted so that they all face the same way, but should be kept separate. Defaced (damaged) notes, and notes from Scotland and Northern Ireland are normally accepted by banks. Coins should normally be sorted into denominations, eg £2, £1, 50p and so on, and placed in plastic money bags.

preparing the cheques

The cheques must first be examined carefully for any irregularities, such as:

- **signatures** – has the issuer signed the cheque?

- **payee** – if the name on the payee line is not the same as the name of the account into which it is being paid, the cheque will not be accepted by the bank

- **date** – is it out of date (over six months old)? is it post-dated (ie does it have a future date)? – if so, it cannot be paid in (but note that you can fill in a missing date and pay in the cheque)

- **words and figures** – are the money amounts the same?

The details of the cheques – the amounts and the customer names – may then be listed on the back of the paying-in slip, as in the illustration on the previous page.

If the number of cheques paid in is very large, there will not be room on the paying-in slip, so the cheque details may be listed on a separate schedule. Some banks accept instead a calculator tally-roll listing the amounts, the number of cheques, and the total money amount transferred to the front of the paying-in slip.

The important point is that the business paying in the cheques must keep a record of the cheque details in case of future queries, and in the unfortunate event of any of the cheques 'bouncing' – ie being returned unpaid.

reconciliation with the financial records

It is important that the paying-in slips are reconciled with the relevant financial and accounting records before the slips are taken to the bank. For example, the total of the paying-in slip could be agreed with the receipts shown in the cash book. Further reconciliations could be carried out between the cheque total and the remittance list and the cash total with the total taken from the cash tills. These reconciliations will highlight any errors – either in the records or on the paying-in slip.

paying in at the bank

At the bank the completed paying-in book is handed to the bank cashier together with the notes, coins, and cheques. The cashier counts the cash, ticks off the cheques and, if everything is correct, receipt stamps and initials the paying-in slip and counterfoil. The slip is retained by the bank for the amount to be credited to the account-holder, while the paying-in book is handed back, complete with the stamped up counterfoil. A business paying-in book is sometimes larger than the paying-in slip illustrated, and there may be a carbon copy which acts as a counterfoil.

security measures for cash handling – night safes

Care must be taken when taking large amounts of cash to the bank. If possible two staff members should visit the bank. If the amount is very large, for instance the takings from a department store, a security firm may be employed to carry the cash. If the cash is received by a business over the weekend or, late in the day, it may be placed in a special wallet and lodged in the bank's **night safe** – a small lockable door leading to a safe in the wall of the bank.

When a business pays in money to the bank, it will record the amount in its own records, the cash book.

CARD VOUCHER CLEARING – CARD MERCHANT SERVICES

As we saw in the last chapter, a sales voucher is the basic document which may be produced when a debit card and a credit card transaction are processed manually, although this is now very rare. The sales voucher may be produced as a result of an 'over-the-counter' sale or from a mail order or telephone sale. The details recorded on it will enable the card company to charge the amount to their customer's bank account (debit card transaction) or credit card account. The voucher, like a cheque, is paid in at the bank and sent to the card company and 'cleared'.

Although there are a number of different card companies – Mastercard and Visa for example – the normal practice is for the business accepting payment to sign an agreement with a separate company – the card merchant – which will accept all vouchers from cards issued by different companies. For example, a customer of The Royal Bank of Scotland (RBS) may sign an agreement with a company called Streamline (owned by The Royal Bank of Scotland) and accept payment by Mastercard and Visa and other cards.

The customer will pay in all credit card vouchers on the one paying-in slip and schedule (see below) at the The Royal Bank of Scotland or NatWest (owned by The Royal Bank of Scotland). The bank will pass them to Streamline, which will then process them by sending them to the issuing card company (Mastercard or Visa, for example). Streamline is only one of a number of 'card merchant' companies which will process credit card sales vouchers.

preparing card sales vouchers for paying in

The vouchers are paid in after completion of a three-part Retailer Summary, illustrated below and on the next page. In this case three sales vouchers are listed on the back of the summary.

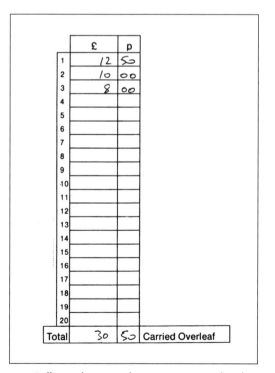

retailer sales voucher summary – back

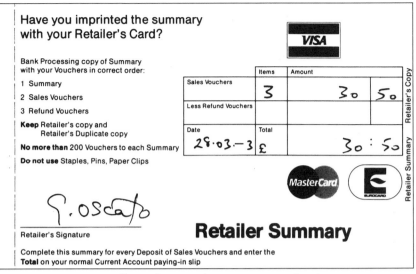

retailer sales voucher summary – front

The procedure for listing credit card sales vouchers on the retailer's summary is as follows:

- the summary is imprinted with details of the retailer using a plastic card – the Retailer's Card – supplied with the imprinter machine

- the amounts of the sales vouchers are listed on the reverse of the summary and totalled

- the total is carried forward to the front of the summary

- any refund vouchers are listed on the front of the summary

- the summary is dated, signed and totalled

- the summary is separated into its three copies – the top two are retained by the business and the bottom copy (the processing copy) is placed in front of the sales vouchers

- the processing copy and sales and any refund vouchers are placed in a transparent envelope and are paid into the bank on a paying-in slip, the total from the summary listed as a single item on the paying-in slip

Businesses which accept sales by mail and telephone may use schedules rather than sales vouchers for recording and listing the credit card transactions. The procedure for paying-in for these businesses is exactly the same, except that the totals of the schedule(s) are listed on the back of the retailer summary rather than the individual amounts of the sales vouchers as described above.

As mentioned earlier, paper-based vouchers and summaries are becoming very rare as credit and debit card transactions are now transmitted electronically from card terminals and checkouts. This electronic process is faster, cheaper and far more efficient.

THE IMPORTANCE OF PAYING IN PROMPTLY

Businesses are well aware that problems can arise if money is not banked promptly and safely.

theft

Cash is tempting to a thief, and it must be remembered that many instances of theft are carried out by employees of a business rather than by criminals from the outside. A business will therefore have a security policy, for example:

- cash and cheques being paid in are kept under lock and key at the place of work, normally in a cash box, under the control of the cashier

- amounts received through the post or over the counter are recorded on remittance lists or on a cash register (or equivalent) as an additional security measure – money, once it is recorded, will be missed when stolen

- larger organisations will have a system of spot checking to identify any theft by employees

- arranging for cash and cheques to be taken to the bank by security firm (appropriate for large businesses)

- arranging for Friday and weekend takings of cash to be lodged in the bank's night safe

timescale – security and cashflow

Businesses will also have a policy for the prompt paying of money into the bank, for two main reasons – **security** and **cashflow**. Money kept on the premises is a security risk: the longer it remains there, the more likely it is that it will be stolen. Also, money not paid in is money that is not available for paying cheques and other items from the business's bank account: cashflow will be restricted. For example, it may be that the business is borrowing money on overdraft – it could save paying interest if money is banked promptly: a cheque for £100,000 lying around in the office for a week could cost the business a significant sum in lost interest!

procedures

Because of these factors a business will draw up procedures for banking money. These will include the security measures mentioned above and also set timescales for paying in money, eg twice a week. If you work in an accounts office, you may be familiar with these procedures.

confidentiality

If you work for an organisation, the importance of confidentiality will have been impressed on you. Confidentiality basically means not telling outsiders about the internal workings of your place of work. Important aspects of this include not talking to outsiders about your customers, not disclosing secret details of your products, and most importantly to this area of your studies, not disclosing your security arrangements for handling of money. Imagine the possible consequences of telling a group of friends that the cash security van calls at the bank every day at 12.00 noon.

AUTOMATED PAYMENTS INTO THE BANK

So far in this chapter we have looked at how a business pays into the bank manually, ie paying in on a paying-in slip. Many payments nowadays come into the bank account by computer transfer from other banks. The business will know about these payments because:

• it will receive notification either through the post or by email

• the payments will appear on the bank statement (see page 50)

A business will enter details of cash and cheque payments in the accounts when the money is received. Payments received electronically must also be entered in the accounts when notification is received and checked in due course against the bank statement. The diagram below shows the variety of payments that can be received. The mechanics of making these payments are covered in Chapter 4.

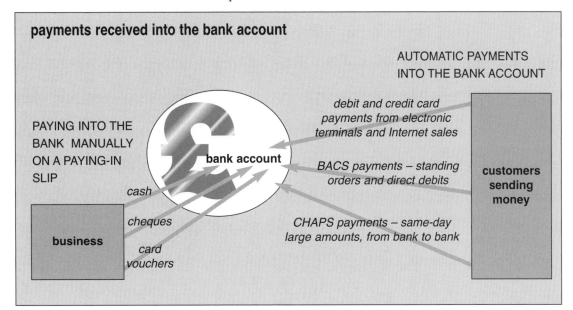

payments received into the bank account

AUTOMATIC PAYMENTS
INTO THE BANK ACCOUNT

PAYING INTO THE
BANK MANUALLY
ON A PAYING-IN
SLIP

bank account

debit and credit card payments from electronic terminals and Internet sales

BACS payments – standing orders and direct debits

CHAPS payments – same-day large amounts, from bank to bank

customers sending money

cash

cheques

card vouchers

business

PAYMENTS THROUGH THE INTERNET

the process

If a business has an internet shopping facility, its customers order and pay for goods or services online using a credit or debit card and the money is credited direct to the bank account of the business. The business will receive a schedule of the payments received which it can check against its bank statement.

The diagram below shows the procedure adopted for this process. There is nothing significantly different from other payment systems about the way this system works – it is merely another way of providing a shopping outlet to customers with debit cards and credit cards.

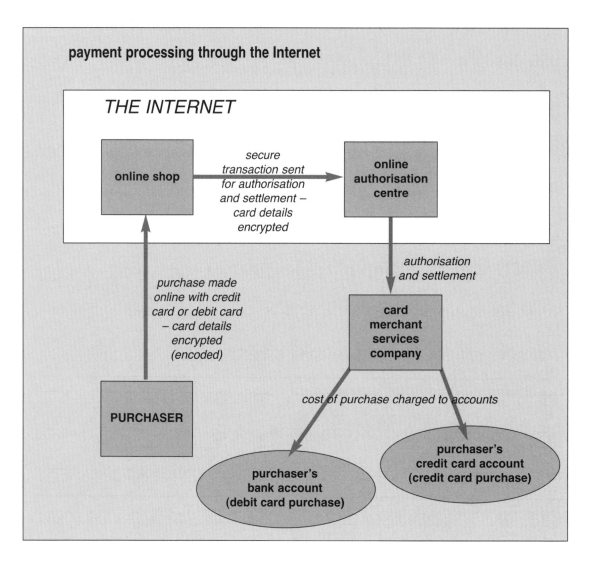

payment processing through the Internet

As we noted in the last chapter, the buying public is concerned about the security of giving their names, addresses and card numbers online. Businesses setting up selling facilities online have to make sure that the security of the system is maintained by using software which encodes the data (data 'encryption') so that payment details remain secret.

This security is no different in principle from the security measures adopted by businesses which accept debit and credit card payments over the counter, ie to keep any records of customers and their card numbers under lock and key and not to throw copies of sales vouchers (with card numbers on) in the bin where they can easily be found.

BANK STATEMENTS

At regular intervals the bank sends out statements of account to its customers or provides them online. A business current account with many items passing through it may have weekly statements, while a less active account or a deposit account may have monthly or even quarterly statements.

A bank statement is a summary showing:

- the balance of the account at the beginning of the statement
- amounts paid into (credited to) the account
- amounts paid out of (debited to) the account – eg cheques issued, cheques returned 'unpaid', bank charges and standing orders and direct debits (automatic computer payments)

The balance of the account is shown after each transaction. A specimen bank statement is shown on the next page.

a note on debits, credits and bank accounts

You should be aware of the fact that the terms 'credit' and 'debit' mean different things to banks and their customers.

In the double-entry system of a business customer

debit = money received

credit = money paid out

Banks see things from the opposite angle. To their accounting system:

debit = money paid out from a customer's account

credit = money paid into a customer's account

In other words a credit to a bank account is the same as a debit in the books of a customer. Think about it!

Albion Bank plc
7 The Avenue, Broadfield, BR1 2AJ

		Account title	Trends
		Account number	11719512
		Statement	85

Date	Details	Payments	Receipts	Balance
20-3				
3 Nov	Balance brought down			1,678.90 CR
10 Nov	Giro Credit 109626		1,427.85	3,106.75 CR
10 Nov	238628	249.57		2,857.18 CR
11 Nov	238629	50.00		2,807.18 CR
13 Nov	POS Streamline		67.45	2,874.63 CR
17 Nov	Giro Credit 109627		100.00	2,974.63 CR
17 Nov	Albionet Card Services POS 2824242		500.00	3,474.63 CR
21 Nov	238630	783.90		2,690.73 CR
24 Nov	238626	127.00		2,563.73 CR
24 Nov	Albionet Netsales 43182639		1,006.70	3,570.43 CR
25 Nov	BACS ORLANDO 37646		162.30	3,732.73 CR
25 Nov	DD Westmid Gas	167.50		3,565.23 CR
27 Nov	238634	421.80		3,143.43 CR
27 Nov	DD RT Telecom	96.50		3,046.93 CR
28 Nov	Bank charges	87.50		2,959.43 CR

checking the bank statement for payments received

You will see from the specimen bank statement shown above that the balance of the account is followed each time by the abbreviation 'CR'. This means that the customer has a credit balance, ie has money in the bank. The abbreviation 'DR' would indicates a debit balance – an overdraft, ie the customer would owe the bank money.

Note the following payments that have been received during the month:

- on 10 and 17 November the business has paid in on a paying-in slip
- on 13 November payment is received from debit card transactions
- on 17 November payment is received from credit card transactions
- on 24 November payment is received from Internet sales
- on 25 November payment is received via the BACS electronic transfer system – possibly a customer settling up an invoice

When a bank statement is received it should be checked and compared with the firm's record of bank receipts and payments – the cash book – and a bank reconciliation statement prepared (see Chapter 6).

- Organisations pay money into their bank account on a paying-in slip which lists the cash and cheques paid in and totals the amounts.

- Cash and cheques must be checked and listed before they are paid in.

- Credit and debit card vouchers may also be paid into the bank account on a retailer summary form which lists all of the vouchers.

- Organisations should set up procedures to ensure that cash, cheques and card vouchers are kept safely on the premises and in transit to the bank.

- Money should be paid into the bank as soon as possible, both for security reasons and also to help the cashflow of the business.

- Automated payments – BACS, CHAPS and card payments processed electronically over the counter and through the internet are also received into the bank account and will be advised to the business.

- Businesses should keep records of automatically processed card payments secure for security reasons – card numbers are valuable to thieves.

- Bank statements are provided to customers and should be checked regularly for manual and automatically processed payments received.

- To a bank, money paid in is a 'credit' and money paid out is a 'debit.'

paying-in slip	a paper slip listing cash and cheques paid into a bank
retailer summary	a form listing credit card sales vouchers paid into a bank account
night safe	a wallet containing cash and cheques lodged with a bank (when it is closed) through an opening in the wall of the bank – used by businesses banking their takings out of hours
card merchant	a company which handles all the payments by debit card and credit card received by a business over the counter or through the Internet
encryption	the encoding for security reasons of debit and credit card details sent over the Internet
BACS	Bankers Automated Clearing Services – used for sending computer payments from bank to bank
CHAPS	Clearing House Automated Payment System – used for sending same-day high value payments
bank statement	a document provided to its customer setting out transactions on the bank account

Activities

3.1 When checking a cheque for paying in at the bank and finding a problem, a business is able to alter the cheque by:

(a) adding the signature of the issuer (drawer) of the cheque if it is missing

(b) changing the amount in words if it is different from the amount in figures

(c) adding the date if it is missing

(d) changing the name of the payee if it is incorrect

Which one of these options is correct?

3.2 The firm you work for is Eveshore Traders Ltd., which has a bank account at Barclays Bank, Eveshore. You are required to prepare the paying-in slip and counterfoil (see below) as at today's date. The cheques are to be listed and totalled on the back of the paying-in slip.

The items to be banked are:

Cash	Cheques	
two £20 notes	£20.00	Maytree Enterprises
five £10 notes	£18.50	Bakewell Catering
eight £5 notes	£75.25	Henderson & Co
two £1 coins	£68.95	Musgrave Fine Art
six 50p coins		
four 10p coins		
two 2p coins		

Date _____	Date _____	**bank giro credit**	£50 notes		
Credit _____	Cashier's stamp and initials		£20 notes		
£50 notes		**Code no** 20 23 88	£10 notes		
£20 notes		**Bank** BARCLAYS	£5 notes		
£10 notes		**Branch** EVESHORE	£1 £2		
£5 notes			50p		
£1 £2		EVESHORE TRADERS LTD	20p		
50p		Credit _____	10p,5p		
20p		Account No. 90003174	Bronze		
10p,5p			Total Cash		
Bronze		**Number of cheques** Paid in by _____	Cheques etc		
Total Cash					
Cheques etc		Do not write below this line	**£**		
£		20-23-88 90003174 77			

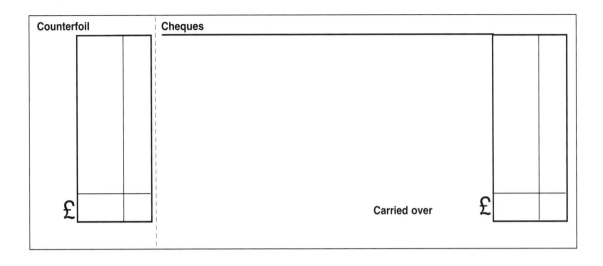

3.3 The firm you work for is Buxton Fine Wines, which has a bank account at Western Bank, Grantminster. Using today's date you are required to prepare the Retailer Summary and paying-in slip for ten credit card sales vouchers and a refund voucher. The documents are shown below and on the next page. The items to be banked are:

Sales vouchers	£45.60	£56.85
	£10.00	£56.00
	£15.50	£45.00
	£25.99	£49.50
	£67.50	£25.00
Refund voucher	£13.50	

Date _____	Date _____	**bank giro credit** ⟳	£50 notes	
Credit _____	Cashier's stamp and initials		£20 notes	
£50 notes		Code no 47 21 95	£10 notes	
£20 notes		Bank ___ WESTERN ___	£5 notes	
£10 notes		Branch ___ GRANTMINSTER ___	£1 £2	
£5 notes			50p	
£1 £2		BUXTON FINE WINES	20p	
50p	Credit	87163729	10p,5p	
20p	Account No. ___		Bronze	
10p,5p			Total Cash	
Bronze		Paid in by ___	Cheques etc	
Total Cash	**Number of cheques**			
Cheques etc		Do not write below this line	£	
£	47 21 95 87163729 77			

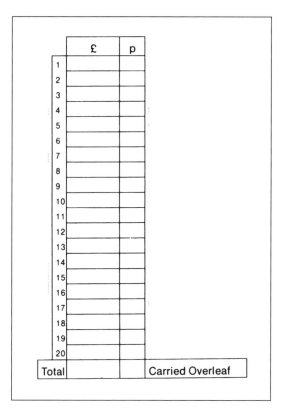

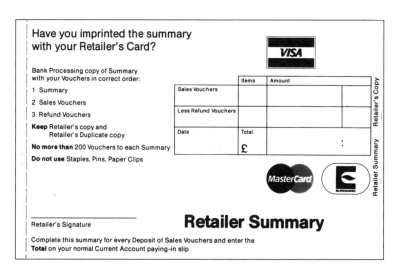

3.4 The firm you work for is Freshmead Limited, which has a bank account at Albion Bank, Broadfield.

You have just received the November bank statement, which is shown below.

Study the statement and answer the questions that follow.

Albion Bank plc
7 The Avenue, Broadfield, BR1 2AJ

	Account title	Freshmead Limited
	Account number	12098525
	Statement	22

Date	Details	Payments	Receipts	Balance
20-3				
3 Nov	Balance brought down			2,678.90 CR
10 Nov	Giro Credit 173406		1,427.85	4,106.75 CR
10 Nov	712518	249.57		3,857.18 CR
11 Nov	712519	50.00		3,807.18 CR
13 Nov	Giro Credit 173407		67.45	3,874.63 CR
17 Nov	Giro Credit 173408		100.00	3,974.63 CR
17 Nov	BACS R Patel 98423		500.00	4,474.63 CR
21 Nov	712520	783.90		3,690.73 CR
24 Nov	712516	127.00		3,563.73 CR
24 Nov	Hermes Netsales 91879184		3,006.70	6,570.43 CR
25 Nov	BACS J Smith Ltd 37646		162.30	6,732.73 CR
25 Nov	DD Ion Power	167.50		6,565.23 CR
27 Nov	712524	421.80		6,143.43 CR
27 Nov	DD Mercury Telecom	96.50		6,046.93 CR
28 Nov	Bank charges	87.50		5,959.43 CR

(a) How much money is there in the account at the beginning of the month and at the end of the month?

(b) Identify the transactions which involve money being paid in on a paying in slip. What is the total paid in?

(c) Identify the transactions which involve cheques issued by Freshmead Limited. What is the total paid out in this way?

(d) Explain what the BACS items on 17 and 25 November are.

(e) What BACS direct debits have been paid out during the month?

(f) What money has been received from Freshmead's online sales for the month?

(g) The opening balance on 3 November is £2,678.90 CR. What would it mean if the statement had shown an opening balance of £2,678.90 DR? What effect would this have had on the bank balance during the month and how would this have been shown on the statement?

4 Making payments

this chapter covers...

We have already seen in Chapter 2 the procedures carried out when a business receives payments from its customers.

This chapter explains the different ways in which payments are prepared and made by a business settling expenses and paying its suppliers. The chapter sets out the procedures followed to make sure that payments are authorised and that confidentiality is maintained. The chapter covers the specific areas of:

- *making payments by cheque*

- *making payments by giro credit inter-bank transfer (paper-based)*

- *making payments by BACS inter-bank transfer (computer-based):*

  - *standing orders*

  - *direct credits*

  - *direct debits*

- *making same-day inter-bank transfers (computer-based):*

  - *CHAPS (for large sums)*

  - *Faster Payments Service (for smaller sums)*

Another system of payment is the making of low-value petty cash payments. This is covered in full in Chapter 7.

OUTGOING PAYMENTS

If you work for an organisation, you will know that there are different types of payments involved; some will involve the issue of cheques or cash, some will involve paying money from the organisation's bank account direct to the recipient's bank account, others will involve paying wages and salaries. Here are some typical examples of these different forms of payment:

issue of cheques

- paying suppliers by cheque for goods and services against invoices and statements
- paying for 'one-off' items of **capital** expenditure, eg a computer system
- paying bills by cheque and bank giro credit
- making small one-off 'cash' purchases

paying through the bank account

- paying wages
- paying regular suppliers for goods and services
- paying bills

PAYING TRADE SUPPLIERS

internal procedures

Each business or organisation will have its own policies and regulations laid down to ensure that payments to suppliers of goods and services are only made when the goods and services have been received as ordered. A supplier of goods and services is therefore paid when:

- the documents relating to the transaction – the purchase order, delivery note (or goods received note) and invoice have been checked against each other (they are normally filed together)
- any credit due, eg for returned goods, has been received in the form of a credit note
- all discounts, whether **settlement (cash) discount** (for early payment) or **trade discount** or **bulk discount** have been identified and allowed for
- the payment has received the necessary authorisation – often in the form of a manager's initials on the invoice, or a rubber stamp

timescales – when to pay?

Each business will also have its own policies and regulations dictating *when* payment is to be made.

payment on invoice – diary system

Businesses often pay strictly according to the due date of the invoice. Each invoice (and all the accompanying documentation), when it is received will be marked with the due date of payment – eg 30 days after the invoice issue date – and placed in a diary system. With this system a business may make individual payments to different suppliers on any number of days of the month. The system is best suited to small businesses which do not have too many payments to make.

payment runs – based on statements

Another widely adopted system is for suppliers to be paid regularly on the basis of the monthly statement issued rather than in response to individual invoices. A business using this system will set up **payment runs** – ie days on which payments will be made during the month. This might be once a month on the last day of the month, or it could be on the second and last Friday of the month – it is up to the business to decide. On each payment run date the supplier statements will be examined and outstanding items paid (unless they are disputed). This system is easy to manage, particularly if the payments are computerised (see below) as only a limited number of payment runs are needed each month to originate either computer-printed cheques or BACS (inter-bank) payments.

payment schedule and remittance advices

We have already seen that the remittance advice tells the supplier what is being paid, either:

- by **cheque**, in which case the remittance advice accompanies the payment, or
- by **BACS** (inter-bank computer payment), in which case the remittance advice is sent separately by post, fax, or by email

If your job is to make payments and prepare remittance advices, you will probably have a **schedule** of payments to work from, with the payment amount already decided upon and authorised by a supervisor.

paying by cheque

If you are paying a supplier you should attach the cheque to the remittance advice. This may be a tear-off slip attached to the supplier's statement of account, or it may be a standard form used within your organisation. An example of the latter is illustrated on the next page and an example of a cheque on page 60. You should note that the following details are shown:

- the date of the payment
- the amount of the cheque
- the details – ie the reference number ('your reference') and date – of the invoice(s) being paid
- the details (reference number and date) of any credit notes deducted
- the purchaser's order number ('our reference')
- the account number of the buyer (from the sales ledger of the seller)

In addition the remittance advice may show further details such as the cheque number and the amount of any settlement (cash) discount deducted for early settlement (there is none in the illustration).

TO	REMITTANCE ADVICE	FROM
Cool Socks Limited **Unit 45 Elgar Estate,** **Broadfield, BR7 4ER**		**Trends** **4 Friar Street** **Broadfield** **BR1 3RF**
Account 3993 31 October 20–3		Tel 01908 761234 Fax 01908 761987 VAT REG GB 0745 8383 56

date	your reference	our reference	payment amount
01 10 20–3 10 10 20–3	INVOICE 787923 CREDIT NOTE 12157	47609 47609	277.30 (27.73)
		CHEQUE TOTAL	249.57

a remittance advice accompanying a cheque payment

payment of suppliers by BACS

The use of BACS, the inter-bank computer payment system, will be dealt with in detail later in the chapter. All BACS payments must be communicated to the supplier by means of a posted, faxed, or emailed remittance advice, otherwise the supplier will not know that payment has been made until the bank statement is received, and even then it may be difficult to identify the origin of the payment. If the supplier does not know payment has been received, he or she may start chasing up the debt, which could prove embarrassing!

ISSUING OF CHEQUES

Cheques may be either completed manually, or printed out on a computer printer.

When writing out (using ink, not pencil) or printing out the cheque you should take care to complete the following:

- correct date
- name of the payee (person receiving the money)
- amount in words
- amount in figures (which should be the same as the amount in words!)
- authorised signature (it may be your signature, it may be that of a manager)
- counterfoil (date, amount, payee)

No room should be left on the cheque for possible fraudulent additions or alterations; any blank spaces should be ruled through. If any errors are made when you are writing out the cheque, they should be corrected and an authorised signature placed close to the alteration in order to tell the bank that it is an approved correction.

tear off cheque here

Date *31/10/-3*	**Albion Bank PLC**	Date *31 October 20-3*	**90 47 17**
	7 The Avenue		
Pay	Broadfield BR1 2AJ		
Cool Socks Limited	Pay *Cool Socks Limited*		
	Two hundred and forty nine pounds 57p A/c payee only	**£ 249.57**	
		TRENDS	
£ 249.57		*V Williams*	
238628	**238628 90 47 17 11719512**		

counterfoil · *cheque*

Computer cheque printing is increasingly used by organisations which use computer accounting programs with a purchase ledger facility. The computer will automatically indicate payments that are due and, subject to authorisation, print out the remittance advice and cheque together, ready for posting. Clearly the computer involved must be closely controlled – and probably password protected – in order to prevent unauthorised access and fraudulent payments.

PAYING FOR 'ONE-OFF' ITEMS – CHEQUE REQUISITION FORMS

So far we have described how to pay trade suppliers who supply on a regular basis for the normal activities of a business, eg manufacturers of crisps who pay farmers for potatoes supplied. The procedure for the issue of cheques in this case is reasonably straightforward. There will be times, however, when a cheque is needed for a 'one-off' purpose, for example:

- purchase of an item of equipment, authorised by the business
- reimbursement of 'out-of-pocket' expenses incurred by an employee
- payment of a pro-forma invoice (a pro-forma invoice is a request for payment to be made before the supply of the goods or services – for example if the customer is a new one)

The normal procedure in these cases is the completion of a **cheque requisition form** by the person who needs the cheque. The example below shows a request for a cheque needed in advance for placing an advert.

Mercia Pumps Limited
CHEQUE REQUISITION FORM

Required by ..**Tom Paget**... Department..**Marketing**.........

CHEQUE DETAILS
date for cheque...**31 March 20-3**..
payable to ...**Media Promotions Limited**...
amount £ ....**360.00**...
despatch to (if applicable)...**Media Promotions Limited, 145 High Street,**
....**Mereford, MR1 3TF**....................................

reason...........**Advert in trade journal**...................general ledger code.....**7556**............

DOCUMENTATION
invoice attached/to follow...**invoice 24516**...
receipt attached/to follow..
other...

AUTHORISATION .....*Andrew Wimbush, Marketing Director*...........date...*31 March 20-3*...........

---

a cheque requisition form

Note the following details on the cheque requisition form:

- the cheque has been ordered by Tom Paget, but is to be sent direct to Media Promotions Limited
- the requisition is authorised by Andrew Wimbush, the Marketing Director
- the invoice is attached
- the general ledger code is included – this is the category of expense for which an account is maintained in the computer accounting system of the business – 7556 is the computer account number for 'advertising account'; if the business did not have a computer accounting system the name of the account in the general ledger – 'advertising' – would be entered

CONTROL AND AUTHORISATION OF PAYMENTS

spending limits

In order to avoid fraud or unchecked spending within a business, all payments must be controlled and authorised. We have seen that incoming invoices must normally be stamped, and signed or initialled by an authorised person before being passed for payment. This is part of an overall system whereby no payment can be made without the necessary authority. The system will vary from business to business, but the following elements will usually be found:

- the larger the payment, the more senior the person who needs to authorise it; often each level of management has a money limit imposed – for example a new vehicle will need to be authorised by senior management
- when an item of expenditure is authorised, the person giving their authority will sign or initial and date the supporting document, eg an invoice, a cheque requisition form

cheque signatures

While a business will have an internal system of signing for and authorising expenditure, it will also have a written agreement with the bank – a bank mandate – which will set out who can sign cheques. A limited company may, for example, allow one director to sign cheques up to £5,000, but will require two to sign cheques in excess of £5,000. It is common to have a number of people authorised to sign to allow for directors going on holiday, going off sick or being away from the office and unavailable for signing cheques.

cash payments

Most businesses will keep a cash float – petty cash – to allow for small everyday items of expenditure such as stationery, postage stamps and other small items of business expense. This is covered in Chapter 7.

PAYING BY BANK GIRO CREDIT

We have already seen in the last chapter how money can be paid into a bank account by means of a bank paying-in slip. So far we have looked at a business which pays in at its own branch, and receives the money in the account on the same day. The banking system also allows for a **bank giro credit** to be paid in at one branch and processed through a three day clearing system to another bank or branch. The bank credit clearing system is widely used for:

- paying bills (electricity, gas, telephone)
- settling credit card accounts

The preprinted bank giro credit is usually a tear-off slip at the bottom of a bill. The person or business paying the bill will fill in:

- the amount of the payment
- the date that the payment is being made at the bank
- in some cases the signature of the person paying in the credit at the bank

The bill is then taken to the bank and paid in, together with a cheque for the appropriate amount. A water bill is shown below.

a bank giro credit

BACS PAYMENTS

Bankers Automated Clearing Services (BACS) is a computer transfer payment system owned by the banks. It is widely used for regular payments such as insurance premiums, settlement of trade debts, wages and salaries. BACS is a cheap and efficient means of payment because, instead of a piece of paper having to be prepared and despatched, the transfer is set up on a computer file and transferred between the banks' computers – the payment goes direct from account to account.

The payment cycle is three working days. If a business wants its suppliers or employees to have the money in their accounts on Friday, the money must leave the business's account on Wednesday. The payment instructions will need to be received by the middle of Wednesday afternoon, so the accounts department will need to observe this deadline.

STANDING ORDERS AND BACS

The business that needs to make regular payments, eg a loan repayment, completes a written authority (a mandate – see below) instructing the bank what payments to make, to whom, and when. The bank then sets up the instructions on its computer, and the payments are made automatically by computer link – using BACS – on the due dates.

STANDING ORDER MANDATE

To _National_ Bank

Address _45 High Street, Hightown, HT1 7FG_

PLEASE PAY TO

Bank _Western_ Branch _Radstock_ Sort code _33 09 87_

Beneficiary _Mendip Loan Brokers_ Account number _29384729_

The sum of _£ 100.00_ Amount in words _one hundred pounds only_

Date of first payment _1 April 20-3_ Frequency of payment _1st monthly_

Until _1 March 20-8_ Reference _FTL294231_

Account to be debited _Janus Limited_ Account number _22472434_

SIGNATURE(S) .... _Archie Rice_ ....

If it is a business which is setting up the standing order, it is important that the mandate form is signed by a person (or persons) authorised to do so – it will often be the person(s) authorised to sign cheques.

BACS DIRECT CREDITS

Businesses often need to make regular payments of **variable** amounts, eg:

- paying wages on pay day
- making payments to established suppliers at the end of each month

The banks have established a BACS **direct credit** system to process these variable payments. Whenever the payments are due to be paid the business sends the bank a schedule (faxed or sent electronically) setting out the details of the payments.

setting up a direct credit system

To set up a direct credit system the bank needs written instructions from the customer before the amounts can be deducted from the account. The details needed by the bank are:

- the name of the 'beneficiary' – the business or person that is to receive the money, eg supplier, employee, insurance company, hire purchase company, etc
- the details of the beneficiary's bank:
  - bank branch
  - sort code number
  - bank account number
- a unique reference number for each beneficiary which is used each time payment is to be made

operating a direct credit system

At the end of each month, for example, the accounts department might draw up a list of the suppliers to be paid and a schedule of employees to be paid. These details will need checking and authorising before instructions are given to the bank. All the business has to do each time payment is to be made is to complete and send to the bank a schedule setting out the payment date, the people being paid, their reference number and the amount – an example is shown on the next page. The schedules may be sent to the bank by post, fax, telephone, or more commonly these days by online instructions. The bank will then process these details through its computers, and payments will be made automatically via the BACS system on the due date.

Case Study	# PAYING SUPPLIERS BY DIRECT CREDIT

1.850

City Traders is a fashion shop based in Mereford. To help the business cut the costs of paying its suppliers the bank has suggested its Direct Credit system. City Traders has provided the suppliers' banking details (sort code and account number) together with an identifying payee reference number in advance for the bank to enter in its computer system. City Traders then writes the monthly payment details on the bank schedule shown below, which is faxed to the bank on Wednesday 24 September. The suppliers will be paid on Friday 26 September.

Mercian Bank PLC
Direct Credit Schedule

Bank branch...Mereford...........................

Originator name.City Traders...........................reference...07246...........

Date ..24/9/20-3

Branch	Account no	Name	Payee no	Amount
45-45-62	10386394	Trendsetters	234	250.00
56-67-23	22347342	FitMan Delivery Co	344	129.76
40-47-07	42472411	Jamesons Ltd	634	450.67
76-87-44	56944491	R Patel	123	409.79
33-00-77	23442413	R D Little Ltd	264	305.78
59-99-01	46244703	Mazzini Import Company	197	560.85
			PAYMENT TOTAL	2106.85

Please make the above payments to reach the payees on ....26/9/20-3...........(date)

Please debit account no......87620261..........with the sum of £...2106.85...............

authorised signature......*D.Craig*...........................

BACS DIRECT DEBITS

The direct debit system is useful for businesses such as insurance companies that receive a large number of variable payments:

- direct debits can be used for either fixed and variable amounts and/or where the time intervals between payments vary

- it is the receiver (beneficiary) of the payment who prepares the computer instructions that request the payer's bank account for payment through the banking system; a direct debit is like a standing order or direct credit operating backwards

paper-based direct debit instructions

The traditional procedure for setting up a direct debit is for the customer making payment to complete and sign a written authority (mandate) prepared by the beneficiary (the person getting the money, eg an insurance company); this is then returned to the beneficiary (eg the insurance company). The payment details are then posted off or sent electronically to the beneficiary's bank so that the computer instructions can be set up. The original form is then returned to the payer's bank. An example of a direct debit mandate is shown below.

DIRECT Debit

Tradesure Insurance Company
PO Box 134, Helliford, HL9 6TY

Originator's Identification Number 914208

Reference (to be completed by Tradesure Insurance) .... 03924540234 ....

Please complete the details and return this form to Tradesure Insurance

name and address of bank/building society

| National Bank plc |
| Market Street |
| Netherway |
| MR7 9YT |

account name

| Grecian Travel Services |

instructions to bank/building society

- I instruct you to pay direct debits from my account at the request of Tradesure Insurance Company.
- The amounts are variable and may be debited on various dates.
- I understand that Tradesure Insurance Company may change the amounts and dates after giving me prior notice.
- I will inform the bank/building society if I wish to cancel this instruction.
- I understand that if any direct debit is paid which breaks the terms of this instruction, the bank/building society will make a refund.

account number	sort code	signature(s)	date
10318736	76 54 29	M Callapolos	1 April 20-3

AUDDIS and the paperless direct debit

Setting up a paper-based direct debit can be a protracted and expensive process, open to error and delay. As a consequence BACS now allows the direct debit payment details to be sent electronically by a system known as AUDDIS (Automated Direct Debit Instruction Service).

AUDDIS is used:

- by businesses such as insurance companies to send direct debit details (received in **writing** from customers) **electronically** to the customer's bank for validation - this system is therefore only partly 'paperless'

- to set up direct debit instructions from customers without using any paper instructions at all, eg the online completion of a direct debit mandate by a customer – this is the **paperless direct debit**

An example of the **paperless direct debit** is a customer wanting to set up a direct debit for an insurance policy on the insurance company's website. Using the AUDDIS system, the customer does not have to sign anything. The instructions (including bank account number, account name and bank sort code) are input by the customer online on the screen and passed electronically to the insurance company. The details are then sent electronically to the banking system – to the insurance company's bank for setting up and then to the customer's bank for approval and validation.

an internet screen for accepting AUDDIS instructions

OTHER 'ONE-OFF' PAYMENTS

In addition to the regular payments processed by BACS standing orders and direct debits, businesses can make 'one-off' payments using the bank computer systems; these include the CHAPS system and the Faster Payments Service. Bank drafts are also widely used for large amount secure payments.

CHAPS

The CHAPS (Clearing House Automated Payments System) payment system is for high value same-day payments sent by the banks through their computer networks. The payment may be in sterling or in euros. CHAPS is used extensively by solicitors when they are arranging the purchase and sale of property for clients. CHAPS payments cannot be cancelled after they have been sent.

Faster Payments Service

In 2008 the main banks and building societies launched the **Faster Payments Service**, the aim of which is to enable customers to send same-day payments from their account to another account at a bank or building society which participates in the scheme. Features of the service include:

- customer instructions for payment may be given at the bank branch, by telephone or over the internet
- customer instructions include the name of the account to receive the payment, the account number, the sort code and any identifying reference number
- the customer must have enough money in the account for the payment
- the payment will normally take only two hours to reach its destination account; once the payment has been sent it cannot be cancelled
- the bank sending the payment will receive an acknowledgement that the payment has been made when it reaches its destination account; if there is a problem with the payment at the receiving bank it will be rejected and the sending bank will be notified

The **Faster Payments Service** is intended for smaller and medium-sized amounts. Larger amounts are normally sent by CHAPS.

bank drafts

A business may have to make a large purchase – for example new vehicles – and be asked to pay by bank draft. A bank draft is a cheque written out by a bank. It is a guaranteed means of payment which is as good as cash, but without the security risks.

COMPANY CREDIT CARDS

Many businesses, particularly those which employ travelling sales representatives, set up a company credit card scheme. This convenient and useful scheme allows company representatives to have credit cards for paying expenses related to the company's business, eg rail tickets, accommodation and food. The credit card bill is settled by the company which is then able to monitor the expenses incurred by its employees.

ONLINE BANKING

With the growth of the use of the internet, many banks are encouraging their customers to manage their payments online. Electronic banking schemes allow customers:

- to get balances and view past transactions
- to print out statements
- to make payments from one account to another
- to set up standing orders

This makes day-to-day management of the finances of a business much simpler. The bank accounts can be monitored 24 hours a day, and greater control can be exercised over payments and receipts.

Chapter Summary

- Outgoing payments made by a business include payments to suppliers, payment of bills, cash payments, 'one-off' items and wages.

- Before paying a supplier a business must see that all procedures and timescales are observed.

- Businesses often pay suppliers at the end of the month, they pay on receipt of the statement rather than in response to individual invoices.

- When making payment by cheque or by BACS a business will normally send the supplier a remittance advice.

- Care must be taken when issuing cheques to ensure that the details are correct and that no room is left on the cheque for fraudulent alterations.

- If an employee needs a cheque for a 'one-off' payment, he or she will need to have a cheque requisition form completed and authorised.

■ The issue of cheques should be strictly controlled through a system of signing 'limits'; normally the larger the amount, the more senior the signatory and the greater the number of signatures required.

■ Payments may be made through the inter-bank transfer system either in paper form or through computer links.

■ Bank giro credits, which take three working days to reach their destination account, are preprinted and are used for paying bills and settling credit card accounts.

■ Bank computer-based payments are made through Bankers Automated Clearing Services (BACS). These also take three working days to clear.

■ A standing order is authorised by the customer in writing and instructs the bank to make regular BACS payments to the beneficiary.

■ If a business needs to send a number of BACS payments on a regular basis but with differing amounts each time – eg when paying regular suppliers – it can authorise the bank to set up a BACS direct credit system. All it needs to do each month is to complete a bank schedule listing the amounts due and the accounts to which they have to be sent.

■ A BACS direct debit is authorised by the customer in writing, over the telephone or the internet and instructs the bank to allow the beneficiary to take sums of money through the BACS from the customer's bank account.

■ AUDDIS (Automated Direct Debit Instruction Service) allows direct debit customer instructions to be captured electronically (eg online) and sent to the paying and receiving banks without the need for any paper documentation.

■ Further methods of bank-to-bank computer payment include:
  – CHAPS (computer inter-bank same day payments, usually for large amounts)
  – the Faster Payments Service for smaller amounts

■ Other more traditional methods of payment include:
  – company credit cards for use by employees for expenses
  – bank drafts (bank cheques which are 'as good as cash')

■ The growth of internet banking has given businesses greater control and flexibility over making payments, and at the same time has allowed them to monitor their bank accounts more closely.

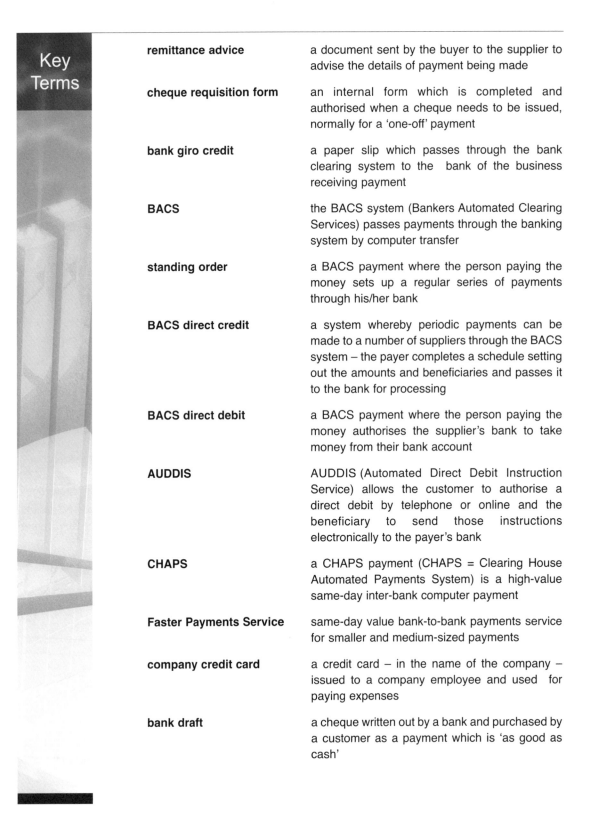

Key Terms

remittance advice	a document sent by the buyer to the supplier to advise the details of payment being made
cheque requisition form	an internal form which is completed and authorised when a cheque needs to be issued, normally for a 'one-off' payment
bank giro credit	a paper slip which passes through the bank clearing system to the bank of the business receiving payment
BACS	the BACS system (Bankers Automated Clearing Services) passes payments through the banking system by computer transfer
standing order	a BACS payment where the person paying the money sets up a regular series of payments through his/her bank
BACS direct credit	a system whereby periodic payments can be made to a number of suppliers through the BACS system – the payer completes a schedule setting out the amounts and beneficiaries and passes it to the bank for processing
BACS direct debit	a BACS payment where the person paying the money authorises the supplier's bank to take money from their bank account
AUDDIS	AUDDIS (Automated Direct Debit Instruction Service) allows the customer to authorise a direct debit by telephone or online and the beneficiary to send those instructions electronically to the payer's bank
CHAPS	a CHAPS payment (CHAPS = Clearing House Automated Payments System) is a high-value same-day inter-bank computer payment
Faster Payments Service	same-day value bank-to-bank payments service for smaller and medium-sized payments
company credit card	a credit card – in the name of the company – issued to a company employee and used for paying expenses
bank draft	a cheque written out by a bank and purchased by a customer as a payment which is 'as good as cash'

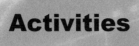

Activities

4.1 The BACS remittance advice is normally attached to the cheque sent in settlement of an account. True or false?

4.2 Why should a cheque not be completed in pencil?

4.3 A cheque requisition form is used for which *one* of the following purposes?

(a) ordering a new cheque book

(b) stopping a cheque

(c) providing specimen signatures to the bank

(d) requesting a cheque within a business

4.4 Explain why a limited company business has to sign a bank mandate.

4.5 (a) What is the difference between a standing order and a direct debit?

State whether a standing order or a direct debit is the better method for the following payments, and why:

(b) a repayment of a fixed loan: £125 per month for five years

(c) a monthly insurance premium which is likely to increase over the years.

4.6 Name two commonly-used methods suitable for making high value 'one-off' payments:

(a) a paper-based payment

(b) a computer-based payment

4.7 Company credit cards are a popular means of making payment.

(a) State one advantage to the employee of the company credit card.

(b) State one advantage to the employer of the company credit card.

For the remainder of the Activities in this chapter you are to take the role of an assistant in the Accounts Department of Nimrod Drainage Limited (a VAT-registered company). Part of your day's work is the preparation of remittance advices and cheques for payments to suppliers. You are not required to sign the cheques. The date is 30 April 20-3.

4.8 Your line manager, Ivor Cash, hands you on 30 April a list of authorised invoices from Jaeger Building Supplies which you are to pay. The monthly payment date is always the last working day of the month. Calculate the amount of the cheque you will have to make out to send with the remittance advice. You do not need to complete any documents.

invoice date	payment terms	invoice total (£)
31 March	30 days	125.89
2 April	30 days	14,658.95
3 April	2.5% cash discount for settlement within 7 days	345.50
9 April	30 days	125.00

4.9 Your line manager hands you a statement from Mercia Wholesalers, Unit 12 Riverside Industrial Park, Mereford MR2 7GH, with a note, indicating the following invoices to be paid, and a credit note to be set off against payment:

Invoice 8765 dated 12 March 20-3, your order number 5517, £765.25

Invoice 8823 dated 2 April 20-3, your order number 5792, £3,567.80

Credit note CN 3420 dated 25 April 20-3 (your ref R/N 5168), £250.00

Complete the remittance advice and cheque set out below. Note that the total of the credit note should be shown in the money column in brackets, indicating that it is a deduction from the payment.

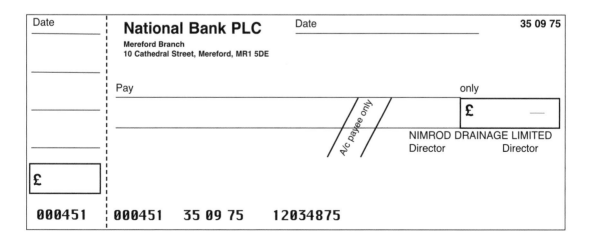

4.10 As an accounts assistant at Nimrod Drainage Limited you have to process the documentation for a wide variety of payments to employees, suppliers and for other business expenses such as one-off purchases, travel costs and bills.

What method of payment would you <u>normally</u> expect to use for the following:

(a)   paying wages to employees who have a bank account

(b)   paying the electricity bill which is sent to the business every three months

(c)   buying a new Porsche car for the Managing Director

(d)   paying travelling expenses for sales representatives

(e)   sending £800,000 to a firm of solicitors for the purchase of new premises

4.11 The date is 30 April 20-3. Your supervisor, Ivor Cash, hands you two documents (shown on the next two pages):

• a blank standing order form provided by the bank

• a direct debit instruction received from Tradesure Insurance Company

Ivor is in rather a rush and asks you to process the two documents, and to return them to the appropriate address with a compliments slip. He also leaves you a piece of paper with written instructions:

Note from: Ivor   30 April 20-3

Hire Purchase Payments

12 monthly instalments of £350 to Broadbent Finance from 15 May 20-3, under reference BE/6637.

Bank details Barclays, Eveshore, 30 98 15, Account 72627161.
Debit our Account 12034875

You are to:

(a)   complete the forms as required (look at the Nimrod Drainage cheque on the previous page for the banking details such as the sort code and account number)

(b)   state to which address you will send them

(c)   describe any other procedure which you may have to carry out before sending off the forms

Note that as an accounts assistant you are not authorised to sign cheques or other payment instructions.

STANDING ORDER MANDATE

To _____ Bank

Address _____

PLEASE PAY TO

Bank _____ Branch _____ Sort code [ ]

Beneficiary Account number [ ]

The sum of £[ ] Amount in words _____

Date of first payment _____ Frequency of payment _____

Until _____ Reference _____

Account to be debited [ ] Account number [ ]

SIGNATURE(S) ....

.... date...........................

DIRECT Debit

Tradesure Insurance Company

PO Box 134, Helliford, HL9 6TY

Originator's Identification Number 914208

Reference (to be completed by Tradesure Insurance) ...... 03924540234 ....

Please complete the details and return this form to Tradesure Insurance

name and address of bank/building society

----

account name

instructions to bank/building society

- I instruct you to pay direct debits from my account at the request of Tradesure Insurance Company.
- The amounts are variable and may be debited on various dates.
- I understand that Tradesure Insurance Company may change the amounts and dates after giving me prior notice.
- I will inform the bank/building society if I wish to cancel this instruction.
- I understand that if any direct debit is paid which breaks the terms of this instruction, the bank/building society will make a refund.

account number   sort code

signature(s)   date

5 Cash book

In this chapter we look at the cash book, the purpose of which is to record the money transactions of a business, such as receiving payments from customers, and making payments to suppliers and for other expenses. Such money transactions are received and paid either in cash, by cheque, BACS (the bank computer payment transfer system), debit or credit card.

We see how the cash book fits into the accounting system as the book of prime entry for money transactions and as part of the double-entry system.

The first layout of the cash book we will look at has money columns for bank, cash and settlement discount. We see how to total and balance this cash book.

Following on from this, we look at an analysed cash book which divides receipts and payments between a number of categories and so provides more information to a business.

Note:
In this chapter we will use the following International Accounting Standards terms:
- *'receivable' – a term which has the same meaning as 'debtor' or 'customer'*
- *'payable' – a term which has the same meaning as 'creditor' or 'supplier'*

Remember:
- *a **receivable** is the person involved where a business will **receive** money*
- *a **payable** is the person involved where a business will have to **pay** money*

THE CASH BOOK IN THE ACCOUNTING SYSTEM

The purpose of the cash book is to record the money transactions of the business. It is the book of prime entry for bank and cash receipts and payments.

In the accounting system, the cash book may combine the roles of the book of prime entry and double-entry book-keeping. This means that the cash book is:

- the book of prime entry for bank and cash receipts and payments
- the double-entry account for bank and cash (kept in general ledger)

The alternative accounting system is where the cash book is used only as the book of prime entry. This requires a separate bank control account (see pages 90-91) and cash control account to be kept in general ledger in order to complete double-entry book-keeping.

Note that, as well as the cash book, businesses often have a petty cash book which is used for low-value cash payments for purchases and expenses. We will study petty cash book in Chapter 7.

USES OF THE CASH BOOK

The cash book records the money transactions of the business, such as:

- receipts
  - from cash sales
  - from receivables (debtors/customers)
  - VAT refunds
  - for other receipts
- payments
  - for cash purchases
  - to payables (creditors/suppliers)
  - for VAT payments
  - for expenses and other payments

Note that the cash book is the record kept by the business of its bank transactions – the bank will keep its own records, and bank statements will either be sent regularly or will be available online through internet banking.

The cash book is controlled by the cashier who:

- records receipts and payments through the bank and in cash
- makes cash payments, and prepares cheques and bank transfers for signature by those authorised to sign

- pays cash and cheques received into the bank
- has control over the business cash – in a cash till or cash box
- issues cash to the petty cashier who operates the petty cash book (see Chapter 7)
- checks the accuracy of the cash and bank balances at regular intervals

It is important to note that transactions passing through the cash book must be supported by documentary evidence. In this way a link is established that can be followed through the accounting system to ensure that it is complete:

- financial document
- book of prime entry
- double-entry accounts

Such a link is required both as a security feature within the business (to help to ensure that false and fraudulent transactions cannot be made), and also for taxation purposes.

The cashier has an important role to play within the accounting function of a business – most business activities will, at some point, involve a money transaction of either a receipt or a payment. Thus the cash book and the cashier are at the hub of the accounting system. In particular, the cashier is responsible for:

- issuing receipts for cash (and sometimes bank transfers) received
- making authorised payments in cash and by cheque/bank transfer against documents received (such as invoices and statements) showing the amounts due

At all times, payments can only be made by the cashier when authorised to do so by the appropriate person within the business, eg the accounts supervisor or the purchasing manager.

With so many transactions passing through the cash book, accounting procedures must include:

- security – of cash, cheque books and internet banking, the correct authorisation of payments
- confidentiality – that all cash/bank transactions, including cash and bank balances, are kept confidential

If the cashier has any queries about any transactions, he or she should refer them to the accounts supervisor.

LAYOUT OF THE CASH BOOK

Although a cash book can be set out in many formats to suit the requirements of a particular business, a common format is the columnar cash book. This is set out in the same way as a double-entry account, with debit and credit sides, but there may be several money columns on each side. An example of a three column cash book (three money columns on each side) is shown below:

Dr							Cash Book					Cr
Date	Details	Ref	Discount allowed	Cash	Bank	Date	Details	Ref	Discount received	Cash	Bank
			£	£	£				£	£	£
			money in						money out		

Note the following points:
- the cash and bank columns on the debit side are used for receipts
- the cash and bank columns on the credit side are used for payments
- on both the debit and credit sides there are separate money columns for cash receipts/payments and bank receipts/payments
- a third money column on each side is used to record settlement (cash) discount (that is, an allowance offered for quick settlement of the amount due, eg 2% cash discount for settlement within seven days)
- the discount column on the debit side is for discount allowed to customers
- the discount column on the credit side is for discount received from suppliers
- the discount columns are not part of the double-entry system – they are used in the cash book as a listing device or memorandum column; as we will see in the Case Study which follows, the discount columns are totalled and transferred into the double-entry system
- the reference column is used to code or cross-reference to the other entry in the double-entry system

Two Case Studies are included in this chapter. The first, below, uses the three column cash book; the second, on page 87, includes use of the analysis columns.

Two Case Studies are included in this chapter. The first, below, uses the three column cash book; the second, on page 87, includes use of the analysis columns.

Case Study

1.850

1.600

CASH BOOK

situation

The following transactions are to be recorded in the three column cash book of Zofia Studios for the month of April 20-7:

1 April	Balances at start of month: cash £300, bank £550
4 April	Received a cheque from T Wright, a customer, for £98 – we have allowed her £2 cash discount
7 April	Paid a cheque to J Crane, a supplier, for £145 – deducting £5 cash discount
11 April	Paid wages in cash £275
14 April	Paid by cheque the account of T Lewis £120, deducting 2.5% cash discount
17 April	J Jones settles in cash her account of £80, deducting 5% cash discount
21 April	Withdrew £100 in cash from the bank for use in the business
23 April	Received a BACS transfer for £45 from D Whitmore in full settlement of her account of £48
28 April	Paid cash of £70 to S Ford in full settlement of our account of £75
30 April	The cash book is balanced and the balances carried down to 1 May

All cheques are banked on the day of receipt.

solution

The cash book records these transactions (as shown on the next page) and, after they have been entered, is balanced on 30 April and the balances carried down to 1 May. (The other part of each double-entry book-keeping transaction is not shown here, but has to be carried out in order to record the transactions correctly.)

Dr												
						Cash Book						**Cr**
Date	Details	Ref	Discount allowed	Cash	Bank	Date	Details	Ref	Discount received	Cash	Bank
			£	£	£				£	£	£
20-7						20-7					
1 Apr	Balances b/d			300	550	7 Apr	J Crane		5		145
4 Apr	T Wright		2		98	11 Apr	Wages			275	
17 Apr	J Jones		4	76		14 Apr	T Lewis		3		117
21 Apr	Bank	C		100		21 Apr	Cash	C			100
23 Apr	D Whitmore		3		45	28 Apr	S Ford		5	70	
						30 Apr	Balances c/d			131	331
			9	476	693				13	476	693
1 May	Balances b/d			131	331						

Note that the transaction on 21 April (£100 withdrawn from the bank for use in the business) involves a transfer of money between cash and bank. As each transaction is both a receipt and a payment within the cash book, it is usual to indicate both of them in the reference column with a 'C' – this stands for 'contra' and shows that both parts of the transaction are in the same book.

BALANCING THE CASH BOOK

At regular intervals, often at the end of each month, the cash book – like the other accounts in the double-entry system – needs to be balanced in order to show the running total of the account. For cash book, it is the cash and bank columns that are separately balanced in order to show:

• the amount of cash held by the business

• the amount of money in the bank (or an overdraft – see below)

The cash book is balanced in the following way (using the cash book, above, as an example):

• add the two cash columns and subtotal in pencil (ie £476 in the debit column, and £345 in the credit column); remember to erase the subtotals afterwards

• deduct the lower total from the higher (payments from receipts) to give the balance of cash remaining (£476 – £345 = £131)

• the higher total is recorded at the bottom of both cash columns in a totals 'box' (£476)

- the balance of cash remaining (£131) is entered as a balancing item above the totals box (on the credit side), and is brought down underneath the total on the debit side as the opening balance for next month (£131)
- the two bank columns are dealt with in the same way (£693 – £362 = £331)

Notice that, in the cash book shown on the previous page, the cash and bank balances have both been brought down on the debit side. It may happen that the balance at bank is brought down on the credit side: this occurs when payments exceed receipts, and indicates a bank overdraft. It is very important to appreciate that the bank columns of the cash book represent the firm's own records of bank transactions and the balance at bank – the bank statement may well show different figures (see the next chapter).

A cash balance can be brought down only on the debit side, indicating the amount of cash held.

At the end of the month, each discount column is totalled separately – no attempt should be made to balance them. At this point, amounts recorded in the columns and the totals are not part of the double-entry system. However, the two totals are transferred into the general ledger in the double-entry system as described below.

discount allowed

From cash book the total of the debit side discount column (£9 in the Case Study) is:

- debited to discount allowed account
- credited to sales ledger control account

The entries for these two general ledger accounts are:

GENERAL LEDGER

Dr			**Discount Allowed Account**		Cr
20-7		£	20-7		£
30 Apr	Cash Book	9			

Dr			**Sales Ledger Control Account**		Cr
20-7		£	20-7		£
			30 Apr	Discount allowed	9

This completes the double-entry for discount allowed in general ledger. However, the discount allowed amounts must be recorded in the memorandum accounts of receivables (debtors) in sales ledger. These are shown as follows:

SALES LEDGER

Dr			**T Wright**		Cr
20-7		£	20-7		£
			4 Apr	Discount allowed	2

Dr			**J Jones**		Cr
20-7		£	20-7		£
			17 Apr	Discount allowed	4

Dr			**D Whitmore**		Cr
20-7		£	20-7		£
			23 Apr	Discount allowed	3

discount received

From cash book the total of the credit side discount column (£13 in the Case Study) is:

– credited to discount received account

– debited to purchases ledger control account

The entries for these two general ledger accounts are:

GENERAL LEDGER

Dr			**Discount Received Account**		Cr
20-7		£	20-7		£
			30 Apr	Cash Book	13

Dr		Purchases Ledger Control Account			Cr
20-7		£	20-7		£
30 Apr Discount received		13			

This completes the double-entry for discount received in general ledger. However, the discount received amounts must be recorded in the memorandum accounts of suppliers in purchases ledger. These are shown as follows:

PURCHASES LEDGER

Dr		J Crane			Cr
20-7		£	20-7		£
7 Apr Discount received		5			

Dr		T Lewis			Cr
20-7		£	20-7		£
14 Apr Discount received		3			

Dr		S Ford			Cr
20-7		£	20-7		£
28 Apr Discount received		5			

ANALYSED CASH BOOK

Many businesses use an analysed cash book to provide more information. As well as the columns for discount, cash and bank which we have seen, an analysed cash book divides receipts and payments between a number of analysis columns, such as:

* receipts
    - from cash sales
    - VAT on cash sales and other receipts

- – receipts from receivables (debtors) in the sales ledger
- – other receipts
- • payments
  - – for cash purchases
  - – VAT on cash purchases and other payments
  - – payments to suppliers (purchases ledger)
  - – other payments (including dealing with dishonoured – 'bounced' cheques)

A business will use whatever analysis columns suit it best: the cash book should be adapted to meet the needs of the business in the best possible way.

Case Study

ANALYSED CASH BOOK

situation

Wyvern Auto Spares buys car parts from manufacturers, and sells to local garages and to members of the public. The business is registered for VAT.

The business uses a cash book which analyses receipts and payments as follows:

RECEIPTS	PAYMENTS
bank	bank
cash	cash
discount allowed	discount received
VAT	VAT
cash sales	cash purchases
sales ledger	purchases ledger
other receipts	other payments

The following transactions are to be entered for the first week of December 20-7:

1 Dec	Balances from previous week: cash £255, bank £875
1 Dec	Sales for cash £240 + VAT
1 Dec	A customer, Main Street Garage, settles an invoice for £195, paying by cheque
2 Dec	Paid rent on premises £325 (no VAT) by cheque
2 Dec	Sales for cash £200 + VAT
2 Dec	Paid an invoice for £250 from Boxhall Supplies Ltd (a supplier) by cheque for £240, £10 being deducted for prompt settlement
3 Dec	Transferred £500 of cash into the bank
3 Dec	Paid for office stationery in cash, £40 + VAT

3 Dec   A45 Service Station, settles an invoice for £143, paying £140 by cheque and is allowed £3 discount for prompt settlement

4 Dec   Sales £320 + VAT, received half in cash, and half by cheque

4 Dec   Paid for urgently needed spares in cash, £80 + VAT

5 Dec   Paid an invoice for £155 from Vord Supplies (a supplier) by cheque for £150, £5 being deducted for prompt settlement

5 Dec   Sales for cash £200 + VAT

5 Dec   Paid wages £385 in cash

5 Dec   Balanced the cash book at the end of the week

As cashier to Wyvern Auto Spares Limited, you are to:

• write up the analysed cash book for the week commencing 1 December 20-7

• balance the cash book at 5 December 20-7

The rate of Value Added Tax is 17.5%. All cheques are banked on the day of receipt.

solution

Dr (Receipts)

Date	Details	Ref	Discount allowed	Cash	Bank	VAT	Cash sales	Sales ledger	Other receipts
20-7			£	£	£	£	£	£	£
1 Dec	Balances b/d			255	875				
1 Dec	Sales	GL		282		42	240		
1 Dec	Main Street Garage	SL			195			195	
2 Dec	Sales	GL		235		35	200		
3 Dec	Cash	C			500				
3 Dec	A45 Service Station	SL	3		140			140	
4 Dec	Sales	GL		188	188	56	320		
5 Dec	Sales	GL		235		35	200		
			3	1,195	1,898	168	960	335	
6 Dec	Balances b/d			169	1,183				

Cr (Payments)

Date	Details	Ref	Discount received	Cash	Bank	VAT	Cash purchases	Purchases ledger	Other payments
20-7			£	£	£	£	£	£	£
2 Dec	Rent	GL			325				325
2 Dec	Boxhall Supplies Ltd	PL	10		240			240	
3 Dec	Bank	C		500					
3 Dec	Office stationery	GL		47		7			40
4 Dec	Purchases	GL		94		14	80		
5 Dec	Vord Supplies	PL	5		150			150	
5 Dec	Wages	GL		385					385
5 Dec	Balances c/d			169	1,183				
			15	1,195	1,898	21	80	390	750

Note the following points:

- The analysed cash book analyses each receipt and payment between a number of headings. A business will adapt the cash book and use whatever analysis columns suit it best.

- For transactions involving sales ledger and purchases ledger, no amount for VAT is shown in the VAT columns. This is because VAT has been charged on invoices issued and received and was recorded in the VAT account (via the day books) when the sale or purchase was made.

- The cash and bank columns are balanced in the way described on pages 83-84.

- The discount columns are totalled at the end of the week and are transferred to the double-entry system as follows:

  – discount allowed column total of £3 is debited to discount allowed account and credited to sales ledger control account – both in general ledger

  – discount received column total of £15 is credited to discount received account and debited to purchases ledger control account – both in general ledger

Note also that the discount columns will be recorded in the memorandum accounts contained in:

  – purchases ledger (accounts of suppliers):
    discount received

  – sales ledger (accounts of customers):
    discount allowed

DEALING WITH DISHONOURED CHEQUES

Sometimes a business pays into its bank account a cheque received from one of its customers and that cheque is **dishonoured** ('bounces'). In other words, the customer's bank – for one of a number of reasons – decides that it will not pay the cheque, which will then become an unpaid cheque.

The practical consequence of this is that the cheque is then deducted from the business bank account and sent back to bank of the business which paid it in. It will be shown on the business bank statement as an unpaid cheque in the payments column.

The reason for a bank returning a cheque in this way can vary:

- the cheque may be 'stopped' by the customer

- there may be something technically wrong with it (it may not have been signed)
- the person issuing the cheque may not have enough money in their bank account; in this case the cheque will be returned marked 'refer to drawer' – which often means that the issuer of the cheque (the customer of the business) is in financial difficulty; this is bad news for the business which should have received the money

An unpaid cheque – like any payment – must be recorded in the cash book bank column (credit side) when it is received back from the bank.

HOW CASH BOOK FITS INTO THE ACCOUNTING SYSTEM

Over the past few pages we have looked at a number of bank and cash receipts and payments which are recorded firstly in the cash book and secondly in the ledger system of general ledger, sales ledger and purchases ledger. As the cash book is the first place in the accounting system to record bank transactions, it is a book of prime entry for bank and cash receipts and payments.

In most accounting systems, cash book also performs the function of being a double-entry account – ie a debit entry made in cash book will be recorded on the credit side of another double-entry account. Some accounting systems treat cash book solely as a book of prime entry, in which case separate double-entry accounts – called **cash control account** and **bank control account** – are used in the general ledger.

CASH AND BANK CONTROL ACCOUNT

As noted above, where an accounting system treats cash book solely as a book of prime entry, a cash control account and a bank control account are used in general ledger to complete double-entry. These accounts show the total receipts and payments made in cash or through the bank during the period, together with opening and closing balances.

From the cash book of Zofia Studios, in the Case Study on page 82, the totals of the receipts and payments from the cash and bank columns are entered in cash control account and bank control account as shown on the next page.

Dr						Cash Book					Cr
Date	Details	Ref	Discount allowed	Cash	Bank	Date	Details	Ref	Discount received	Cash	Bank
			£	£	£				£	£	£
20-7						20-7					
1 Apr	Balances b/d			300	550	7 Apr	J Crane		5		145
4 Apr	T Wright		2		98	11 Apr	Wages			275	
17 Apr	J Jones		4	76		14 Apr	T Lewis		3		117
21 Apr	Bank	C		100		21 Apr	Cash	C			100
23 Apr	D Whitmore		3		45	28 Apr	S Ford		5	70	
						30 Apr	Balances c/d			131	331
			9	476	693				13	476	693
1 May	Balances b/d			131	331						

GENERAL LEDGER

Dr		Cash Control Account			Cr
20-7		£	20-7		£
1 Apr	Balance b/d	300	30 Apr	Cash Book	345
30 Apr	Cash Book	176	30 Apr	Balance c/d	131
		476			476
1 May	Balance b/d	131			

Dr		Bank Control Account			Cr
20-7		£	20-7		£
1 Apr	Balance b/d	550	30 Apr	Cash Book	362
30 Apr	Cash Book	143	30 Apr	Balance c/d	331
		693			693
1 May	Balance b/d	331			

Note that the amounts shown as Cash Book on the debit sides of the two control accounts are the total receipts from cash book, excluding balances brought down (and, if applicable, carried down). Likewise, the amounts shown on the credit sides exclude balances brought down (if applicable) and carried down.

CHECKING THE CASH BOOK

As the cash book forms such an integral part of a business double-entry system, it is essential that transactions are recorded accurately and that balances are calculated correctly at regular intervals, eg weekly or monthly – depending on the needs of the business. How can the cash book be checked for accuracy?

cash columns

To check the cash columns is easy. It is simply a matter of counting the cash in the cash till or box, and agreeing it with the balance shown by the cash book. In the example from the cash book of Zofia Studios, in the Case Study on page 82, there should be £131 in the firm's cash till at 30 April 20-7. If the cash cannot be agreed in this way, the discrepancy needs to be investigated urgently.

bank columns

How are these to be checked? We could, perhaps, enquire at the bank and ask for the balance at the month-end, or we could arrange for a bank statement to be sent to us, or we could use internet banking to print off a statement. However, the balance of the account at the bank may well not agree with that shown by the bank columns of the cash book. There are several reasons why there may be a difference: for example, a cheque that has been written out recently to pay a bill may not yet have been recorded on the bank statement, ie it has been entered in the cash book, but is not yet on the bank statement. To agree the bank statement and the bank columns of the cash book, it is usually necessary to prepare a bank reconciliation statement, and this topic is dealt with fully in the next chapter.

Chapter Summary

■ The purpose of the cash book is to record the money transactions of the business in the form of cash and bank receipts and payments.

■ Receipts are recorded on the debit side; payments are recorded on the credit side.

■ A common form of cash book is the three column cash book with money columns for cash, bank, and settlement discount.

■ An analysed cash book provides more information and divides receipts and payments between a number of analysis columns.

■ Cash book may combine the roles of:
  – the book of prime entry for bank and cash receipts and payments
  – the double-entry account for bank and cash

■ When the cash book is used only as the book of prime entry, a cash control account and a bank control account are used in general ledger to complete double-entry book-keeping.

■ The total of the discount allowed column in cash book is transferred to the double-entry system as:
  – debit discount allowed account
  – credit sales ledger control account

■ Discount allowed amounts must also be recorded in the memorandum accounts of receivables (debtors) in sales ledger.

■ The total of the discount received column in cash book is transferred to the double-entry system as:
  – debit purchases ledger control account
  – credit discount received account

■ Discount received amounts must also be recorded in the memorandum accounts of suppliers in purchases ledger.

■ A dishonoured cheque must be recorded in the cash book bank column (credit side) when it is received back from the bank.

cash book	records bank receipts and payments; may combine the roles of the book of prime entry for bank and cash receipts and payments and the double-entry account for bank and cash
three column cash book	cash book with columns for cash, bank, and settlement discount
analysed cash book	divides receipts and payments between a number of analysis columns
discount allowed	amount allowed by a business to its customers who settle amounts due within the period for cash discount stated on the sales invoice
discount received	amount received by a business from its suppliers for quick settlement within the period for cash discount stated on the supplier's invoice
dishonoured cheque	a cheque which is paid into a bank account, but is returned unpaid by the bank; it is then deducted from the account of the business or person that paid it in
cash control account and bank control account	double-entry accounts in general ledger used when cash book is treated solely as the book of prime entry; they show the total receipts and payments made in cash or through the bank during the period, together with the opening and closing balances

Activities

5.1 Which one of the following transactions will not be recorded on the payments side of cash book?

(a) purchase of a vehicle for £10,000 paid for by cheque

(b) cash purchase for £150

(c) cheque received from a customer for £1,350

(d) BACS transfer to a supplier for £2,200

Answer (a) or (b) or (c) or (d)

5.2 Which one of the following transactions will not be recorded on the receipts side of cash book?

(a) cheque paid to a supplier for £870

(b) BACS transfer from a customer for £3,250

(c) debit card payment by a customer for £580

(d) cash sales of £195

Answer (a) or (b) or (c) or (d)

5.3 Indicate whether the following statements are true by putting a tick in the relevant column of the table below.

		True	False
(a)	Cash book is the book of prime entry for bank and cash receipts and payments		
(b)	Cash book can be the double-entry account for bank and cash		
(c)	The discount received column total from cash book is debited to discount received account in general ledger		
(d)	The VAT column total on the receipts side of cash book is debited to VAT account in general ledger		
(e)	The sales ledger column total from cash book is credited to sales ledger control account in general ledger		

5.4   Walter Harrison is a sole trader who records his cash and bank transactions in a three column cash book. The following are the transactions for June 20-2:

1 June	Balances: cash £280; bank overdraft £2,240
3 June	Received a BACS transfer from G Wheaton, a customer, for £195, in full settlement of a debt of £200
5 June	Received cash of £53 from T Francis, a customer, in full settlement of a debt of £55
8 June	Paid the amount owing to F Lloyd, a supplier, by cheque: the total amount due is £400 and Harrison takes advantage of a 2.5% per cent cash discount
10 June	Paid wages in cash £165
12 June	Paid A Morris, a supplier, in cash, £100 less 3 per cent cash discount
16 June	Withdrew £200 in cash from the bank for use in the business
18 June	Received a cheque for £640 from H Watson, a customer, in full settlement of a debt of £670
20 June	Paid R Marks, a supplier, £78 by BACS
24 June	Paid D Farr, a supplier, £65 by BACS, in full settlement of a debt of £67
26 June	Paid telephone account £105 in cash
28 June	Received a BACS transfer from M Perry, a customer, in settlement of his account of £240 – he has deducted 2.5% per cent cash discount
30 June	Received cash £45 from K Willis, a customer

You are to:

(a)   Enter the above transactions in Harrison's three column cash book, balance the cash and bank columns at 30 June, and carry the balances down to 1 July.

(b)   Total the two discount columns and transfer the totals to the discount accounts in general ledger.

5.5 You work for Metro Trading company as an accounts assistant. One of your duties is to write-up the cash book. Metro Trading's cash book is both a book of prime entry and a double-entry account. On 1 August 20-7, the balances in the cash book were:

Cash £276 debit

Bank £4,928 debit

Transactions for the month were:

1 Aug	Received a BACS transfer from Wild & Sons Limited, a customer, £398
5 Aug	Paid T Hall Limited, a supplier, a cheque for £541 in full settlement of a debt of £565
8 Aug	Paid wages in cash £254
11 Aug	Withdrew £500 in cash from the bank for use in the business
12 Aug	Received a cheque for £1,755 from A Lewis Limited, a customer, in full settlement of their account of £1,775
18 Aug	Paid F Jarvis, a supplier, £457 by BACS
21 Aug	Received a cheque for £261 from Harvey & Sons Limited, a customer
22 Aug	Paid wages in cash £436
25 Aug	Paid J Jones, a supplier, a cheque for £628 in full settlement of a debt of £661
27 Aug	Paid salaries by cheque £2,043
28 Aug	Paid telephone account by cheque £276
29 Aug	Received BACS transfer for £595 from Wild & Sons Limited in full settlement of their account of £610
29 Aug	Withdrew £275 in cash from the bank for use in the business

All cheques are banked on the day of receipt.

You are to:

(a) Enter the above transactions in the three column cash book of Metro Trading Company.

(b) Balance the cash and bank columns at 31 August, and carry the balances down to 1 September.

(c) Total the two discount columns.

(d) Show the cash book transactions in the following general ledger accounts:
   – discount allowed account
   – discount received account

(e) Show the discount amounts in the following sales ledger accounts:
   – Wild & Sons Ltd
   – A Lewis Ltd

(f) Show the discount amounts in the following purchases ledger accounts:
   – T Hall Ltd
   – J Jones

5.6 Note: this question has money amounts in pounds and pence.

David Lewis runs a shop selling carpets to the public on cash terms and to trade customers on credit terms. He buys his carpets direct from manufacturers, who allow him credit terms.

David Lewis' business is registered for VAT. He uses an analysed cash book, which is a book of prime entry and a double-entry account.

The following transactions take place during the week commencing 12 May 20-7 (all cheques are banked on the day of receipt):

12 May	Balances from previous week: cash £205.75, bank £825.30
12 May	Cash sales £534.62 (including VAT), cheque received
12 May	Paid shop rent by cheque £255.50 (no VAT)
13 May	Cash sales £164.50 (including VAT), cash received
13 May	A customer, T Jarvis, settles an invoice for £157.50, paying £155.00 by cheque, £2.50 settlement discount being allowed
13 May	Paid an invoice for £368.20 from Terry Carpets (a supplier) by cheque for £363.55 and receiving £4.65 settlement discount
14 May	Cash sales £752.00 (including VAT), cheque received
14 May	Paid an invoice for £149.00 from Trade Supplies (a supplier) for £145.50, paying by cheque and receiving £3.50 settlement discount
14 May	Purchases paid for in cash, £28.20 (including VAT)
15 May	Transferred £250 of cash into the bank
15 May	Cash sales £264.37 (including VAT), cash received
15 May	Paid an invoice for £295.80 from Longlife Carpets (a supplier), by cheque for £291.50 and receiving £4.30 settlement discount
16 May	Cash purchases of £258.50 (including VAT) paid by BACS
16 May	A customer, Wyvern Council, settles an invoice for £565.45, paying £560.45 by BACS and is allowed £5.00 discount for prompt settlement

You are to:

(a) Enter the above transactions in the analysed cash book of David Lewis shown on the next page (VAT amounts should be rounded down to the nearest penny).

(b) Balance the cash book at 16 May 20-7.

(c) Explain how the totals for the discount columns will be entered in the accounts in the general ledger (the general ledger accounts do not need to be shown).

(d) Show the discount transactions in the following accounts:

sales ledger	–	T Jarvis
	–	Wyvern Council
purchases ledger	–	Terry Carpets
	–	Trade Supplies
	–	Longlife Carpets

The rate of Value Added Tax is 17.5%.

Dr (Receipts)

Date	Details	Ref	Discount allowed £	Cash £	Bank £	VAT £	Cash sales £	Sales ledger £	Other receipts £

Cr (Payments)

Date	Details	Ref	Discount received £	Cash £	Bank £	VAT £	Cash purchases £	Purchases ledger £	Other payments £

6 Bank reconciliation statements

this chapter covers...

The purpose of a bank reconciliation statement is to form the link between the balance at bank shown in the cash book of a business book-keeping system and the balance shown on the bank statement received from the bank.

The reasons why the cash book and bank statement may differ are because:

- *there are timing differences caused by:*
  - *unpresented cheques, ie the time delay between the business writing out a cheque and recording it in the cash book, and the cheque being entered by the bank on the bank statement*
  - *outstanding lodgements, ie amounts paid into the bank by the business, but not yet recorded on the bank statement*
- *the cash book has not been updated with items which appear on the bank statement and which should also appear in the cash book such as direct debits, standing orders and bank charges*

Assuming that there are no errors and both cash book and bank statement are correct, the two documents need to be reconciled with each other, ie their closing balances need to be agreed by means of a calculation known as a bank reconciliation statement.

RECEIVING THE BANK STATEMENT

When the bank statement is received it must be matched or compared with the cash book in order to identify any differences or discrepancies.

These are:

* timing differences
* updating items for the cash book

timing differences

The two main timing differences or discrepancies between the bank columns of the cash book and the bank statement are:

* **unpresented cheques**, ie cheques issued, not yet recorded on the bank statement
* **outstanding lodgements**, ie amounts paid into the bank, not yet recorded on the bank statement

The first of these – **unpresented cheques** – is caused because, when a cheque is written out, it is immediately entered on the payments side of the cash book, even though it may be some days before the cheque passes through the bank clearing system and is recorded on the bank statement. Therefore, for a few days at least, the cash book shows a lower balance than the bank statement in respect of this cheque. When the cheque is recorded on the bank statement, the difference will disappear. We have looked at only one cheque here, but a business will often be issuing many cheques each day, and the difference between the cash book balance and the bank statement balance may be considerable.

With the second timing difference – **outstanding lodgements** – the business's cashier will record a receipt in the cash book as he or she prepares the bank paying-in slip. However, the receipt may not be recorded by the bank on the bank statement for a day or so, particularly if it is paid in late in the day, or if it is paid in at a bank branch other than the one at which the account is maintained.

Until the receipt is recorded by the bank the cash book will show a higher bank account balance than the bank statement. Once the receipt is entered on the bank statement, the difference will disappear.

These two timing differences are involved in the calculation known as the **bank reconciliation statement**. The business cash book must not be altered because, as we have seen, they will correct themselves on the bank statement as time goes by.

updating items for the cash book

Besides the timing differences described on the previous page, there may be other differences between the bank columns of the cash book and the bank statement, and these do need to be entered in the cash book to bring it up-to-date.

For example, the bank might make an automatic standing order payment on behalf of a business – such an item is correctly deducted by the bank, and it might be that the bank statement acts as a reminder to the business cashier of the payment: it should then be entered in the cash book.

Examples of items that show in the bank statement and need to be entered in the cash book include:

receipts - money in

- credit transfers (BACS – Bankers Automated Clearing Services) amounts received by the bank, eg payments from receivables (debtors) - ie customers

- dividend amounts received by the bank

- interest paid by the bank

payments - money out

- standing order and direct debit payments (many businesses keep schedules of their standing orders and direct debits – from these they write up the cash book as the payments fall due)
- bank charges and interest
- unpaid cheques deducted by the bank, for example, cheques from customers paid in by the business which have 'bounced' and are returned by the bank marked 'refer to drawer'

For each of these items, the cashier needs to check to see if they have been entered in the cash book; if not, they need to be recorded (provided that the bank has not made an error). If the bank has made an error, it must be notified as soon as possible and the incorrect transactions reversed by the bank in its own accounting records.

THE BANK RECONCILIATION STATEMENT

The **bank reconciliation statement** forms the link between the balances shown in the bank statement and in the cash book:

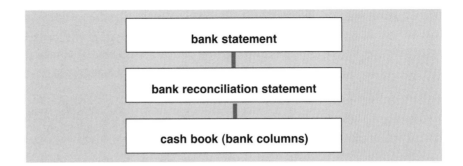

Upon receipt of a bank statement, reconciliation of the two balances is carried out in the following way:

- tick off the items that appear in both cash book and bank statement
- the unticked items on the bank statement are entered into the bank columns of the cash book to bring it up-to-date (provided none are errors made by the bank)
- the bank columns of the cash book are now balanced to find the revised figure
- the remaining unticked items from the cash book will be the timing differences
- the timing differences are used to prepare the bank reconciliation statement, which takes the following format (with example figures):

XYZ TRADING LIMITED
Bank Reconciliation Statement as at 31 October 20-1

		£	£
Balance at bank as per bank statement			245
Less: unpresented cheques			
J Lewis	cheque no 0012378	60	
ABC Limited	cheque no 0012392	100	
Eastern Oil Company	cheque no 0012407	80	
			240
			5
Add: outstanding lodgements		220	
		300	
			520
Balance at bank as per cash book			525

Notes:

- The layout shown above starts from the bank statement balance, and works towards the cash book balance. A common variation of this layout is to start with the cash book balance and to work towards the bank statement balance (see page 108).

- If a bank overdraft is involved, brackets should be used around the numbers to indicate this for the bank statement or cash book balance. The timing differences are still added or deducted, as appropriate.

- Once the bank reconciliation statement agrees, it should be filed because it proves that the bank statement and cash book were reconciled at a particular date. If, next time it is prepared, it fails to agree, the previous statement is proof that reconciliation was reached at that time.

Case Study

BANK RECONCILIATION STATEMENT

situation

The cashier of Severn Trading Company has written up the firm's cash book for the month of February 20-1, as shown below.

Note that the cheque number is shown against payments.

Dr					Cash Book			Cr
Date	Details	Cash	Bank	Date	Details		Cash	Bank
20-1		£	£	20-1			£	£
2 Feb	Balances b/d	250.75	1,340.50	3 Feb	Appleton Ltd 123456			675.25
6 Feb	A Abbott		208.50	5 Feb	Wages		58.60	
10 Feb	Sales	145.25		12 Feb	Rent	123457		125.00
16 Feb	Sales		278.30	17 Feb	D Smith & Co 123458			421.80
20 Feb	Sales	204.35		24 Feb	Stationery		75.50	
23 Feb	D Richards Ltd		162.30	25 Feb	G Christie	123459		797.55
26 Feb	Sales		353.95		Balances c/d		466.25	586.25
27 Feb	P Paul Ltd		262.30					
		600.35	2,605.85				600.35	2,605.85
	Balances b/d	466.25	586.25					

The cash balance of £466.25 shown by the cash columns at the month-end has been agreed with the cash held in the firm's cash box. The bank statement for February 20-1 has just been received:

National Bank plc

Branch .Bartown................

TITLE OF ACCOUNT ..Severn Trading Company.............

ACCOUNT NUMBER ..67812318.............................

STATEMENT NUMBER 45

DATE	PARTICULARS	PAYMENTS	RECEIPTS	BALANCE
20-1		£	£	£
2 Feb	Balance brought forward			1340.50 Cr
7 Feb	Credit		208.50	1549.00 Cr
10 Feb	Cheque 123456	675.25		873.75 Cr
17 Feb	Credit		278.30	1152.05 Cr
17 Feb	Cheque 123457	125.00		1027.05 Cr
24 Feb	Credit		162.30	1189.35 Cr
24 Feb	BACS J Jarvis Ltd		100.00	1289.35 Cr
26 Feb	Cheque 123458	421.80		867.55 Cr
26 Feb	Direct debit A-Z Finance	150.00		717.55 Cr
27 Feb	Credit		353.95	1071.50 Cr
27 Feb	Bank charges	10.00		1061.50 Cr

solution

Note that the bank statement is prepared from the bank's viewpoint: thus a credit balance shows that the customer is a payable (creditor) of the bank, ie the bank owes the balance to the customer. In the customer's own cash book, the bank is shown as a debit balance, ie an asset.

As the month-end balance at bank shown by the cash book, £586.25, is not the same as that shown by the bank statement, £1,061.50, it is necessary to compare individual items in the cash book and on the bank statement for accuracy. The steps are:

1   Tick off the items that appear in both cash book and bank statement.

2   The unticked items on the bank statement are entered into the bank columns of the cash book to bring it up-to-date. These are:

- receipt   24 Feb   BACS credit, J Jarvis Limited £100.00

- payments   26 Feb   Direct debit, A-Z Finance £150.00

           27 Feb   Bank Charges, £10.00

In double-entry book-keeping, the other part of the transaction will need to be recorded in the accounts.

3 The cash book is now balanced to find the revised balance:

Dr		£	20-1		£
20-1					
	Balance b/d	586.25	26 Feb	A-Z Finance	150.00
24 Feb	J Jarvis Ltd	100.00	27 Feb	Bank Charges	10.00
			28 Feb	Balance c/d	526.25
		686.25			686.25
1 Mar	Balance b/d	526.25			

Cash Book (bank columns) — Cr

4 The remaining unticked items from the cash book are:

- receipt 27 Feb – P Paul Limited £262.30

- payment 25 Feb – G Christie (cheque no 123459) £797.55

These items are timing differences, which should appear on next month's bank statement. They will be used in the bank reconciliation statement.

5 The bank reconciliation statement is now prepared, starting with the bank statement balance of £1,061.50 and using the unticked items from the cash book which were noted above.

SEVERN TRADING COMPANY
Bank Reconciliation Statement as at 28 February 20-1

	£
Balance at bank as per bank statement	1,061.50
Less: unpresented cheque, no 123459	797.55
	263.95
Add: outstanding lodgement, P Paul Limited	262.30
Balance at bank as per cash book	526.25

This bank reconciliation statement starts with the bank statement balance, and finishes with the amended balance from the cash book, ie the two figures are reconciled.

notes on the case study

- The unpresented cheque is deducted from the bank statement balance because, until it is recorded by the bank, the bank statement shows a higher balance than the cash book.

- The outstanding lodgement is added to the bank statement balance because, until it is recorded by the bank, the bank statement shows a lower balance than the cash book.

PREPARING A BANK RECONCILIATION STATEMENT

In order to help with the Activities at the end of the chapter, here is a step-by-step summary of the procedure. Reconciliation of the bank statement balance with that shown in the cash book should be carried out in the following way:

1   From the bank columns of the cash book tick off, in both cash book and bank statement, the receipts that appear in both.

2   From the bank columns of the cash book tick off, in both cash book and bank statement, the payments that appear in both.

3   Identify the items that are unticked on the bank statement and enter them in the cash book on the debit or credit side, as appropriate. (If, however, the bank has made a mistake and debited or credited an amount in error, this should not be entered in the cash book, but should be notified to the bank for them to make the correction. The amount will need to be entered on the bank reconciliation statement.)

4   The bank columns of the cash book are now balanced to find the up-to-date balance.

5   Start the bank reconciliation statement with the final balance figure shown on the bank statement.

6   In the bank reconciliation statement deduct the unticked payments shown in the cash book – these will be unpresented cheques.

7   In the bank reconciliation statement, add the unticked receipts shown in the cash book – these are outstanding lodgements.

8   The resulting money amount shown on the bank reconciliation statement is the balance at bank as per the cash book.

The layout which is often used for the bank reconciliation statement is that shown in the Case Study on the previous page. The layout starts with the bank statement balance and finishes with the cash book balance. However, there is no reason why it should not commence with the cash book balance and finish with the bank statement balance: with this layout it is necessary to:

*   *add* unpresented cheques
*   *deduct* outstanding lodgements

The bank reconciliation statement of Severn Trading Company would then appear as (see the next page):

SEVERN TRADING COMPANY
Bank Reconciliation Statement as at 28 February 20-1

	£
Balance at bank as per cash book	526.25
Add: unpresented cheque, no 123459	797.55
	1,323.80
Less: outstanding lodgement, P Paul Limited	262.30
Balance at bank as per bank statement	1,061.50

DEALING WITH UNUSUAL ITEMS ON BANK STATEMENTS

The following are some of the unusual features that may occur on bank statements. As with other accounting discrepancies, where they cannot be resolved they should be referred to the accounts supervisor for guidance.

out-of-date cheques

These are cheques that are more than six months old. The bank will not pay such cheques, so they can be written back in the cash book, ie debit cash book (and credit the other double-entry account involved).

returned (dishonoured) cheques

A cheque received by a business is entered as a receipt in the cash book and then paid into the bank, but it may be returned ('bounced') by the drawer's (issuer's) bank to the payee's bank because:

- the drawer (the issuer) has stopped it
- the cheque has been returned by the bank, either because the drawer has no money (a 'dishonoured' cheque) or because there is a technical problem with the cheque, eg it is not signed

A cheque returned in this way should be entered in the book-keeping system:

- as a payment in the cash book on the credit side, and
- – either as a debit to sales ledger control account (if it is a credit sale), and a debit to the receivable's (debtor's) account in sales ledger
  - or as a debit to sales account (if it is a cash sale)

bank errors

Errors made by the bank can include:

- **a cheque deducted from the bank account which has not been issued by the business** – look for a cheque number on the bank statement that is different from the current cheque series: take care, though, as it could be a cheque from an old cheque book

* **a BACS receipt shown on the bank statement for which the business is not the correct recipient**; if in doubt, the bank will be able to give further details of the sender of the money

* **standing orders and direct debits paid at the wrong time or for the wrong amounts**; a copy of all standing order and direct debit mandates sent to the bank should be kept by the business for reference purposes, standing order and direct debit schedules should be kept up-to-date so that the cash book can be written up as the payments fall due

When an error is found, it should be queried immediately with the bank. The item and amount should not be entered in the firm's cash book until it has been resolved. If, in the meantime, a bank reconciliation statement is to be prepared, the bank error should be shown separately. When the reconciliation is from the bank statement balance to the cash book balance, add payments and deduct receipts that the bank has applied to the account incorrectly.

bank charges and interest

From time-to-time the bank will debit business customers' accounts with an amount for:

- service charges, ie the cost of operating the bank account
- interest, ie the borrowing cost when the bank account is overdrawn

Banks usually notify customers in writing before debiting the account.

reconciliation of opening cash book and bank statement balances

If you look back to the Case Study on pages 104-105, you will see that both the cash book (bank columns) and the bank statement balance both started the month with the same balance: 1 February 20-1 £1,340.50.

In reality, it is unlikely that the opening cash book and bank statement balances will be the same. It will be necessary, in these circumstances, to prepare a simple opening bank reconciliation statement in order to prove that there are no errors between cash book and bank statement at the start of the month.

This is set out in the same format as the end-of-month bank reconciliation statement, and is best prepared immediately after ticking off the items that appear in both cash book and bank statement. The earliest unpresented cheques drawn and outstanding lodgements will, most probably, be causing the difference. Of course, where last month's bank reconciliation statement is available, such as in business, there is no need to prepare an opening reconciliation.

There is usually no need to prepare a formal opening bank reconciliation statement as any discrepancy in opening balances can be resolved quickly by checking the bank statement for the earliest receipts and payments.

IMPORTANCE OF BANK RECONCILIATION STATEMENTS

- A bank reconciliation statement is important because, in its preparation, the transactions in the bank columns of the cash book are compared with those recorded on the bank statement. In this way, any errors in the cash book or bank statement will be found and can be corrected (or advised to the bank, if the bank statement is wrong).

- The bank statement is an independent accounting record, therefore it will assist in deterring fraud by providing a means of verifying the cash book balance.

- By writing the cash book up-to-date, the business has an amended figure for the bank balance to be shown in the trial balance.

- It is good business practice to prepare a bank reconciliation statement each time a bank statement is received. The reconciliation statement should be prepared as quickly as possible so that any queries – either with the bank statement or in the firm's cash book – can be resolved. Many firms will specify to their accounting staff the timescales for preparing bank reconciliation statements – as a guideline, if the bank statement is received weekly, then the reconciliation statement should be prepared within five working days.

Chapter Summary

■ The purpose of a bank reconciliation statement is to agree the balance shown by the bank statement with that shown by the bank columns of the cash book.

■ Certain differences between the two are timing differences. The main timing differences are:

- unpresented cheques
- outstanding lodgements

These differences will be corrected by time and, most probably, will be recorded on the next bank statement.

■ Certain differences appearing on the bank statement need to be entered in the cash book to bring it up-to-date. These include:

Receipts   – credit transfer (BACS) amounts received by the bank

– dividend amounts received by the bank

– interest credited by the bank

Payments   – standing order and direct debit payments

– bank charges and interest

– unpaid cheques debited by the bank

■ The bank reconciliation statement makes use of the timing differences.

■ Once prepared, a bank reconciliation statement is proof that the bank statement and the cash book (bank columns) were agreed at a particular date.

Key Terms

bank reconciliation statement	forms the link between the balances shown in the bank statement and the cash book
timing differences	discrepancies between the bank statement and the cash book that will be corrected over time, such as unpresented cheques and outstanding lodgements
unpresented cheques	cheques drawn, but not yet recorded on the bank statement
outstanding lodgements	amounts paid into the bank, but not yet recorded on the bank statement
direct debit/standing order schedules	lists of direct debit and standing order payments, kept by a business, from which the cash book is written up as payments fall due

Activities

6.1 When preparing a bank reconciliation statement, which one of the following is a timing difference?

(a)   unpresented cheques

(b)   direct debit payments

(c)   bank charges and interest

(d)   BACS receipts

Answer (a) or (b) or (c) or (d)

6.2 A firm's bank statement shows a balance of £400. Unpresented cheques total £350; outstanding lodgements total £200. What is the balance at bank shown by the cash book?

(a)   £100

(b)   £200

(c)   £250

(d)   £400

Answer (a) or (b) or (c) or (d)

6.3 The bank columns of Tom Reid's cash book for December 20-2 are as follows:

20-2	Receipts		£	20-2	Payments		£
1 Dec	Balance b/d		280	9 Dec	W Smith	345123	40
13 Dec	P Jones		30	13 Dec	Rent	345124	50
17 Dec	H Homer		72	16 Dec	Wages	345125	85
29 Dec	J Hill		13	20 Dec	B Kay	345126	20
				31 Dec	Balance c/d		200
			395				395

He then received his bank statement which showed the following transactions for December 20-2:

BANK STATEMENT		Payments	Receipts	Balance
20-2		£	£	£
1 Dec	Balance brought forward			280 CR
13 Dec	Credit		30	310 CR
15 Dec	Cheque no 345123	40		270 CR
17 Dec	Cheque no 345124	50		220 CR
22 Dec	Credit		72	292 CR
23 Dec	Cheque no 345125	85		207 CR

You are to prepare a bank reconciliation statement which agrees the bank statement balance with the cash book balance.

6.4 The bank columns of P Gerrard's cash book for January 20-3 are as follows:

20-3	Receipts	£	20-3	Payments		£
1 Jan	Balance b/d	800.50	2 Jan	A Arthur Ltd	001351	100.00
6 Jan	J Baker	495.60	9 Jan	C Curtis	001352	398.50
30 Jan	G Shotton Ltd	335.75	13 Jan	Donald & Co	001353	229.70
			14 Jan	Bryant & Sons	001354	312.00
			23 Jan	P Reid	001355	176.50

He received his bank statement which showed the following transactions for January 20-3:

BANK STATEMENT		Payments	Receipts	Balance
20-3		£	£	£
1 Jan	Balance brought forward			800.50 CR
6 Jan	Cheque no 001351	100.00		700.50 CR
6 Jan	Credit		495.60	1,196.10 CR
13 Jan	BACS credit: T K Supplies		716.50	1,912.60 CR
20 Jan	Cheque no 001352	398.50		1,514.10 CR
23 Jan	Direct debit: Omni Finance	207.95		1,306.15 CR
26 Jan	Cheque no 001353	229.70		1,076.45 CR

You are to:

(a)   check the items on the bank statement against the items in the cash book and update the cash book accordingly; total the cash book and show the balance carried down at 31 January 20-3

(b)   prepare a bank reconciliation statement at 31 January 20-3 which agrees the bank statement balance with the cash book balance

6.5   The bank columns of Jane Doyle's cash book for May 20-4 are as follows:

20-4	Receipts	£	20-4	Payments		£
1 May	Balance b/d	300	3 May	P Stone	867714	28
7 May	Cash	162	14 May	Alpha Ltd	867715	50
17 May	C Brewster	89	28 May	E Deakin	867716	110
27 May	Cash	60				
28 May	Cash	40				

She received her bank statement which showed the following transactions for May 20-4:

BANK STATEMENT		Payments	Receipts	Balance
20-4		£	£	£
1 May	Balance brought forward			400 CR
2 May	Cheque no 867713	100		300 CR
5 May	Cheque no 867714	28		272 CR
7 May	Credit		162	434 CR
17 May	Standing order: A-Z Insurance	25		409 CR
19 May	Credit		89	498 CR
20 May	Cheque no 867715	50		448 CR
26 May	Credit		60	508 CR
31 May	Bank Charges	10		498 CR

You are to:

(a)   write the cash book up-to-date at 31 May 20-4, and show the balance carried down

(b)   prepare a bank reconciliation statement at 31 May 20-4 which agrees the bank statement balance with the cash book balance

6.6 On 4 June Milestone Motors received a bank statement which showed the following transactions for May 20-5:

BANK STATEMENT		Paid out	Paid in	Balance
20-5		£	£	£
1 May	Balance brought forward			3,802 C
2 May	Cheque no 451761	150		3,652 C
10 May	Cheque no 451762	751		2,901 C
11 May	Cheque no 451763	268		2,633 C
13 May	Cheque no 451765	1,045		1,588 C
14 May	BACS credit: Perran Taxis		2,596	4,184 C
18 May	Direct debit: Wyvern Council	198		3,986 C
20 May	Direct debit: A1 Insurance	1,005		2,981 C
25 May	Direct debit: Okaro and Company	254		2,727 C
25 May	Bank charges	20		2,707 C
D = Debit C = Credit				

The cash book of Milestone Motors as at 31 May 20-5 is shown below:

CASH BOOK

Date	Details	Bank	Date	Cheque no	Details	Bank
20-5		£	20-5			£
1 May	Balance b/f	3,652	4 May	451762	Smith and Company	751
26 May	J Ackland	832	4 May	451763	Bryant Limited	268
28 May	Stamp Limited	1,119	7 May	451764	Curtis Cars	1,895
			7 May	451765	Parts Supplies	1,045

You are to:

(a)   check the items on the bank statement against the items in the cash book

(b)   update the cash book as needed

(c)   total the cash book and show clearly the balance carried down at 31 May and brought down at 1 June

(d)   prepare a bank reconciliation statement at 31 May 20-5 which agrees the bank statement balance with the cash book balance

6.7 On 27 June Durning Trading received a bank statement as at 27 June 20-8:

BANK STATEMENT		Paid out	Paid in	Balance
20-8		£	£	£
1 Jun	Balance brought forward			768 C
4 Jun	Cheque 364125	427		341 C
5 Jun	BACS credit: Asif Ltd		1,122	1,463 C
18 Jun	Cheque 364127	4,200		2,737 D
20 Jun	Direct debit: JC Property Co	850		3,587 D
23 Jun	BACS credit: Sand & Stone		2,486	1,101 D
26 Jun	BACS credit: Surfrider Ltd		4,110	3,009 C
27 Jun	Direct debit: Vord Finance	275		2,734 C
27 Jun	Cheque 364128	1,062		1,672 C
D = Debit C = Credit				

The cash book of Durning Trading as at 27 June 20-8 is shown below:

CASH BOOK

Date	Details	Bank	Date	Cheque no	Details	Bank
20-8		£	20-8			£
1 Jun	Balance b/d	1,890	1 Jun	364125	Penryn Ltd	427
20 Jun	Chiverton Ltd	1,200	3 Jun	364126	Fal Boats	760
24 Jun	Perran Ltd	4,750	10 Jun	364127	S Mawes	4,200
24 Jun	P Porth	8,950	20 Jun	364128	Castle Supplies	1,062

You are to:

(a) check the items on the bank statement against the items in the cash book

(b) update the cash book as needed

(c) total the cash book and clearly show the balance carried down at 27 June and brought down at 28 June

(d)   using the form below, prepare a bank reconciliation statement as at 27 June which agrees the bank statement balance with the cash book balance (note: not all the lines may be needed)

Bank reconciliation statement as at 27 June 20-8	
Balance as per bank statement	£
Add	
Name:	£
Name:	£
Name:	£
Name:	£
Total to add	£
Less	
Name:	£
Name:	£
Name:	£
Name:	£
Total to subtract	£
Balance as per cash book	£

7 Petty cash book

this chapter covers...

In this chapter we look at the petty cash book, the purpose of which is to record low-value cash payments for small purchases and expenses incurred by a business.

The way that petty cash book works is that an amount of cash is handed by the cashier to a member of staff, the petty cashier, who:

- *is responsible for security of the petty cash money*

- *makes cash payments against authorised petty cash vouchers*

- *records the payments made, and analyses them, in a petty cash book*

- *reconciles the petty cash book with the amount of cash held*

We look at the layout of the petty cash book, with analysis columns for expenses and see how it is written up by the petty cashier from authorised petty cash vouchers.

We see how a petty cash book is balanced and how the petty cashier claims reimbursement from the cashier of amounts of money paid out.

Towards the end of the chapter we will see how a petty cash book fits into the accounting system as a book of prime entry for low-value cash payments and as part of the double-entry system.

THE PETTY CASH PROCEDURE

The purpose of the **petty cash book** is to record low-value cash payments for purchases and expenses – such as small items of stationery, postages, etc. Items like these are not appropriate to be entered in the cash book because they would 'clutter' it up with lots of small amounts. Instead, an amount of cash is handed by the cashier to a member of staff, the petty cashier, who is responsible for all aspects of the control of petty cash, principally:

- security of the petty cash money
- making cash payments against authorised petty cash vouchers
- recording the payments made, and analysing them, in a petty cash book
- reconciling the petty cash book with the amount of cash held

In order to operate the petty cash system, the petty cashier needs the following:

- a petty cash book in which to record and analyse transactions
- a lockable cash box in which to keep the money
- a stock of blank petty cash vouchers (see page 123) for claims on petty cash to be made
- a lockable desk drawer in which to keep these items

making a claim

An employee is most likely to encounter the petty cash system when making claims for money for small purchases that have been made. Before studying the form-filling procedures in detail, read the summary of a typical petty cash transaction set out below:

your supervisor asks you to go and buy a box of pens from an office supplies shop

↓

you go to the shop and buy the pens; having paid for them, you retain the receipt (for £5.50) so that you can claim the money from the petty cashier on your return to the office

↓

your supervisor authorises a petty cash voucher containing details of the purchase; you attach the shop receipt to the petty cash voucher

↓

you hand the authorised petty cash voucher and shop receipt to the petty cashier who gives you £5.50 in cash

↓

the petty cashier enters the details of the petty cash transaction in the petty cash book

WHAT ITEMS CAN BE PASSED THROUGH PETTY CASH BOOK?

Petty cash is used to make small cash payments for purchases and expenses of the business. Examples of petty cash payments include:

- stationery items
- small items of office supplies
- window cleaning
- bus, rail and taxi fares incurred on behalf of the business
- meals and drinks incurred on behalf of the business
- postages
- donations

Petty cash should not be used to pay for private expenses of employees, eg tea, coffee, and milk, unless the business has agreed to pay for these in advance. Usually there will be a list of approved expenses that can be reimbursed from petty cash. All payments made through petty cash must be supported by relevant documentation. This documentation includes:

- receipt from a shop
- post office receipt for postage
- rail or bus ticket
- receipt from taxi company
- receipt from window cleaning firm

The business will decide on the maximum value for any transaction that can be paid out of petty cash – for example, up to £25 is a common authorised limit.

Case Study

1.850

1.600

PETTY CASH EXPENSES

situation

You are employed as an accounts assistant for Tyax Engineering Limited. As a training exercise the accounts supervisor asks you which of the following expenses you would allow to be paid out of petty cash? The upper limit for petty cash transactions is £25.

- envelopes for use in the office, £2.50
- postage on an urgent parcel of engineering parts, £3.75
- bus fare to work claimed by secretary, £2.20
- car mileage to work of office manager called in late at night when the burglar alarm went off (false alarm!), £15.50
- tea and coffee for use in the office, £3.70
- office window cleaning, £6.80

- plant bought for reception area, £5.50
- computer back-up tapes, £35.00
- donation to local charity by the business, £10.00
- meal allowance paid to a member of staff required to work during the lunch hour, £5.00

Note: you may assume that all expenses are supported by relevant documentation, such as receipt from a shop, post office etc.

solution

For most expenses it is clear whether or not they can be drawn from petty cash. However, there are points to consider for some of the expenses.

Envelopes	pay from petty cash
Postage	pay from petty cash
Bus fare to work	this is a personal expense and cannot be drawn from petty cash
Car mileage	travel to work is a personal expense, as seen with the previous item; however, as this expense was a special journey in the middle of the night in order to resolve a business problem, it can be paid from petty cash
Tea and coffee	these cannot be paid out of petty cash, unless the business has agreed to provide them free to its employees; however, if the tea and coffee were used to make drinks for official visitors and customers, they can be paid from petty cash
Window cleaning	pay from petty cash
Plant	pay from petty cash (but plants for the general office cannot be bought with the company's money)
Computer tapes	this is a business expense but, in view of the amount (above the authorised limit of the petty cashier) it is too large to be paid out of petty cash; instead it should be paid from the cash book by the cashier
Donation	pay from petty cash, subject to authorisation by supervisor
Meal allowance	pay from petty cash, provided that it is company policy to make an allowance in these circumstances

Notes to the Case Study

- Before payments can be made for petty cash expenses, they must be:
  - within the limits for a petty cash transaction (for example, £25 maximum for any one transaction)
  - supported by documentary evidence, such as a receipt or a rail/bus ticket
  - authorised by the appropriate supervisor or manager
- If the petty cashier is unable to resolve whether or not an expense can be paid from petty cash, the item should be referred to the accounts supervisor for a decision.

THE IMPREST SYSTEM

Petty cash books usually operate using the imprest system. With this system, the petty cashier starts each week (or month) with a certain amount of money – the imprest amount. As payments are made during the week (or month) the amount of money will reduce and, at the end of the period, the cash will be made up by the main cashier to the imprest amount. For example:

Started week with imprest amount	£100.00
Total of petty cash amounts paid out during week	£80.00
Cash held at end of week	£20.00
Amount drawn from cashier to restore imprest amount	£80.00
Cash at start of next week, ie imprest amount	£100.00

If, at any time, the imprest amount proves to be insufficient, further amounts of cash can be drawn from the cashier. Also, from time-to-time, it may be necessary to increase the imprest amount so that regular shortfalls of petty cash are avoided.

PETTY CASH VOUCHERS

Petty cash vouchers are the financial documents against which payments are made out of petty cash. They are the financial documents used by the petty cashier to write up the petty cash book.

Petty cash vouchers are completed as follows:

- with the date, details and amount of expenditure

- with the signature of the person making the claim and receiving the money

- with the signature of the person authorising the payment to be made – usually the supervisor or the manager of the person making the claim

- additionally, most petty cash vouchers are numbered, so that they can be controlled, the number being entered in the petty cash book

- with the relevant documentation, such as a receipt from a shop or post office etc, should be attached to the petty cash voucher

An example of a petty cash voucher is shown on the next page:

petty cash voucher		number *47*
	date	*8 October 20-4*

description		amount

	£	p
Photocopier paper	*3*	*20*
VAT at 17.5%	*0*	*56*
Total	*3*	*76*

signature   *T Harris*

authorised   *R Singh*

LAYOUT OF THE PETTY CASH BOOK

Petty cash book is usually set out as follows:

Receipts	Date	Details	Voucher number	Total payment	Analysis columns				
					VAT	Postages	Stationery	Travel	Ledger
£				£	£	£	£	£	£
money in: debit side				money out: credit side					

This layout shows that:

- there are columns showing the date and details of all receipts and payments

- receipts are shown in the debit column on the extreme left

- there is a column for the petty cash voucher number

- the total payment (ie the amount paid out on each petty cash voucher) is in the next column, which is the credit side of the petty cash book

- there are analysis columns on the right which analyse each transaction entered in the 'total payment' column

A business will use whatever analysis columns are most suitable for it and, indeed, there may be more columns than shown in the example. It is important that expenses are recorded in the correct analysis columns so that petty cash book shows a true picture of petty cash expenditure.

PETTY CASH AND VAT

Value Added Tax is charged by VAT-registered businesses on their taxable supplies. Therefore, there will often be VAT included as part of the expense paid out of petty cash. Often the indication of the supplier's VAT registration number on a receipt or invoice will tell you that VAT has been charged on the items purchased.

Where VAT has been charged, the amount of tax might be indicated separately on the receipt or invoice. However, for small money amounts it is quite usual for a total to be shown without indicating the amount of VAT. An example of a receipt which does not show the VAT content is illustrated below. The receipt is for a box of envelopes purchased from Wyvern Stationers. It shows:

- the name and address of the retailer

- the date and time of the transaction

- the VAT registration number of the retailer

- the price of the item, £4.70

- the amount of money given, a £10 note

- the amount of change given, £5.30

Wyvern Stationers	
25 High St Mereford	
08 10 -4	**16.07**
VAT Reg 454 7106 34	
Salesperson Rashid	
Stationery	**4.70**
TOTAL	**4.70**
CASH	**10.00**
CHANGE	**5.30**

What the receipt does not show, however, is the VAT content of the purchase price – it only shows the price after the VAT has been added on.

How do we calculate the purchase price before the VAT is added on?

The formula is:

$$\frac{\textbf{amount paid x 100}}{\textbf{100 + VAT rate}} \quad = \quad \textbf{price before VAT is added on}$$

If we assume that the VAT rate is 17.5%, the calculation is

$$\frac{\pounds4.70 \text{ x } 100}{100 + 17.5} \quad = \quad \frac{\pounds470}{117.5} \quad = \quad \pounds4.00$$

The VAT content is therefore

£4.70 minus £4.00 = 70p

In this case £0.70 will be entered in the VAT column in the petty cash book, £4.00 in the appropriate expense column, and the full £4.70 in the total payment column.

Remember when calculating VAT amounts that fractions of a penny are ignored, ie the tax is rounded down to a whole penny.

Case Study

1.850

1.600

PETTY CASH BOOK

situation

You work in the accounts office of Wyvern Traders. One of your tasks is to keep the petty cash book, which is operated using the imprest system. There are a number of transactions which have been authorised (all transactions, unless otherwise indicated, include VAT at 17.5%) to be entered for the week on page 30 of the petty cash book:

20-4

5 Apr	Started the week with an imprest amount of £100.00
5 Apr	Paid stationery £3.76 on voucher no 47
5 Apr	Paid taxi fare £5.64 on voucher no 48
6 Apr	Paid postages £2.75 (no VAT) on voucher no 49
7 Apr	Paid taxi fare £9.40 on voucher no 50
7 Apr	Paid J Jones, a supplier, £15.00 (no VAT shown in petty cash book – amount will be on VAT account already) on voucher no 51
8 Apr	Paid stationery £7.05 on voucher no 52
8 Apr	Paid postages £5.85 (no VAT) on voucher no 53
9 Apr	Paid taxi fare £11.75 on voucher no 54

solution

The petty cash book is written up as follows:

					Analysis columns				
Petty Cash Book									**PCB30**
Receipts	Date	Details	Voucher number	Total payment	VAT	Postages	Stationery	Travel	Ledger
£	20-4			£	£	£	£	£	£
100.00	5 Apr	Balance b/d							
	5 Apr	Stationery	47	3.76	0.56		3.20		
	5 Apr	Taxi fare	48	5.64	0.84			4.80	
	6 Apr	Postages	49	2.75		2.75			
	7 Apr	Taxi fare	50	9.40	1.40			8.00	
	7 Apr	J Jones	51	15.00					15.00
	8 Apr	Stationery	52	7.05	1.05		6.00		
	8 Apr	Postages	53	5.85		5.85			
	9 Apr	Taxi fare	54	11.75	1.75			10.00	
				61.20	5.60	8.60	9.20	22.80	15.00

Notes on the Case Study:

- Each page of the petty cash book is numbered – here 'PCB30' – this helps with cross-referencing in the accounts system.

- For each petty cash item, the analysis columns add up to the amount shown in the 'total payment' column

- The totals of the analysis columns add up to the total payment

- The petty cashier will give details of the total of each analysis column to the appropriate accounts assistant so that the amounts can be recorded in the double-entry accounts system

- Total payments are £61.20 and, as the petty cash book is kept using the imprest system, this is the amount of cash which will need to be drawn from the cashier in order to restore the imprest

- We shall see how the petty cash book is balanced in the next section.

BALANCING PETTY CASH BOOK

A petty cash book is balanced by comparing the receipts and payments columns. Where a petty cash book is operated using the imprest system, a further receipt will be the amount of cash received from the cashier to restore the imprest amount – this is equal to the total paid out during the week.

The following illustration shows how the petty cash book seen in the Case Study on the previous page is balanced at the end of the week:

		Petty Cash Book							PCB30
Receipts	Date	Details	Voucher number	Total payment	Analysis columns				
					VAT	Postages	Stationery	Travel	Ledger
£	20-4			£	£	£	£	£	£
100.00	5 Apr	Balance b/d							
	5 Apr	Stationery	47	3.76	0.56		3.20		
	5 Apr	Taxi fare	48	5.64	0.84			4.80	
	6 Apr	Postages	49	2.75		2.75			
	7 Apr	Taxi fare	50	9.40	1.40			8.00	
	7 Apr	J Jones (PL054)	51	15.00					15.00
	8 Apr	Stationery	52	7.05	1.05		6.00		
	8 Apr	Postages	53	5.85		5.85			
	9 Apr	Taxi fare	54	11.75	1.75			10.00	
				61.20	5.60	8.60	9.20	22.80	15.00
					GL2200	GL6330	GL6360	GL6370	GL2350
61.20	9 Apr	Bank (CB55)							
	9 Apr	Balance c/d		100.00					
161.20				161.20					
100.00	10 Apr	Balance b/d							

Note that, here, the imprest amount of £61.20 has been restored at the end of the week and before the petty cash book has been balanced. An alternative method is to balance the petty cash book *before* restoring the imprest amount – in the above example, this will give a balance brought down on 10 April of £38.80 (ie £100.00 minus £61.20); the money received from the cashier (£61.20) will then be recorded in the receipts column.

The petty cashier will then give details of the total of each analysis column – or pass over the book itself – to the employee who needs to record the totals in the double-entry book-keeping system.

RESTORING THE CASH FLOAT

To restore the petty cash float to the imprest amount, the petty cashier completes a cheque requisition form for a cheque made payable to cash. The petty cashier takes the cheque to the bank and obtains the cash. An example of a cheque requisition is shown below:

CHEQUE REQUISITION	
Amount	*£61.20*
Payee	*Cash*
Date	*9 April 20-4*
Details	*Reimbursement of petty cash*
Signature	*Jane Watkins, petty cashier*
Authorised by	*Natalie Wilson, accounts supervisor*
Cheque no	*017234*

cheque requisition form

The double-entry book-keeping entries to record this reimbursement are:
– *debit* petty cash book
– *credit* cash book, ie the payments side

The amount of £61.20 cash paid to the petty cashier is recorded in the cash book as follows:

Dr							Cash Book			**CB55**		Cr
Date	Details	Ref	Discount allowed	VAT	Bank	Date	Details	Ref	Discount received	VAT	Bank
20-4			£	£	£	20-4 9 Apr	Petty cash	PCB30	£	£	£ 61.20

After this reimbursement, the petty cash float is restored and the petty cash book has a balance carried down on 9 April and brought down on 10 April of £100.00. The petty cash book is now ready for next week's transactions.

CONTROL OF PETTY CASH

The petty cashier is usually responsible to the accounts supervisor for control of the petty cash and for correct recording of authorised petty cash transactions.

Most businesses set out in writing the procedures to be followed by the petty cashier. This is of benefit not only for the petty cashier to know the extent of his or her duties, but also to help the person who takes over at holiday or other times. The main procedures for the operation and control of petty cash are as follows:

1   On taking over, the petty cashier should check that the petty cash book has been balanced and that the amount of cash held agrees with the balance shown in the book. If there is any discrepancy, this should be referred to the accounts supervisor immediately.

2   The petty cashier should ensure that each week or month is started with the imprest amount of cash which has been agreed with the accounts supervisor.

3   The petty cash is to be kept securely in a locked cash book, and control kept of the keys.

4   Petty cash vouchers (in number order) are to be provided on request.

5   Petty cash is paid out against correctly completed petty cash vouchers after checking that:

–   the voucher is signed by the person receiving the money

–   the voucher is signed by the person authorising payment (a list of authorised signatories will be provided)

–   a receipt (or other supporting evidence) is attached to the petty cash voucher, and that receipt and petty cash voucher are for the same amount

–   the amount being claimed is within the authorised limit of the petty cashier

6   The petty cash book is written up (to include calculation of VAT amounts when appropriate); it is important that the petty cash book is accurate.

7   Completed petty cash vouchers are stored safely – filed in numerical order. The vouchers will need to be kept for at least six years. They may be needed by the auditors or in the event of other queries. Completed petty cash books will also need to be retained.

8   A surprise check of petty cash will be made by the accounts supervisor – at any one time the cash held plus amounts of petty cash vouchers should equal the imprest amount.

9   At the end of each week or month the petty cash book is to be balanced.

10   Details of the totals of each analysis column are given to the person who looks after the double-entry accounts so that the amount of each expense can be entered into the double-entry system.

11   An amount of cash is drawn from the cashier equal to the amount of payments made, in order to restore the imprest amount.

12   The petty cash book and cash in hand are to be presented to the accounts supervisor for checking.

13   Any discrepancies are to be dealt with promptly; these may include:

– petty cash claims that have not been authorised

– insufficient supporting evidence (eg missing receipt) attached to the petty cash voucher

– amounts being claimed which exceed the authorised limit of the petty cashier

– a receipt and petty cash voucher total differing – the matter should be queried with the person who made the purchase

– a difference between the totals of the analysis columns and the total payments column in the petty cash book – check the addition of the columns, the figures against the vouchers, the VAT calculations (does the VAT plus the analysis column amount equal the total payment amount?)

– a difference between the cash in the petty cash box and the balance shown in the petty cash book – if this is not an arithmetic difference it may be a case of theft, and should be reported promptly to the accounts supervisor

– where discrepancies and queries cannot be resolved, they should be referred to the accounts supervisor

CHECKING THE CASH

An important aspect of petty cash, which has been noted in the previous section, is that the petty cashier must ensure that the amount of cash held is what it should be. This process – known as reconciling the petty cash book with cash in hand – takes place on different occasions, as follows:

• at the beginning of the weekly or monthly period of the petty cash book, the petty cashier should check that the amount of cash held agrees with the balance shown in the book – this is usually the imprest amount

- at any one time during the week or month the amount of cash held plus the amounts of petty cash vouchers which have been paid out should be equal to the imprest amount – a surprise check may be made by the accounts supervisor

- at the end of the week or month, the amount paid out by the petty cashier will be reimbursed from cash book – this should restore the cash in hand to the imprest amount

Any difference in cash – whether a shortfall or a surplus – at any stage during the week or month should be investigated promptly and, if it cannot be resolved, should be referred to the accounts supervisor.

Case Study

CHECKING THE CASH

situation

Jameson Limited keeps an amount of petty cash in a locked box in the office. The imprest amount is £100 which is restored at the beginning of each month.

The following payments were made in April and have been recorded in the petty cash book:

6 April	Stationery	£12.50
10 April	Taxi fare	£10.00
14 April	Postage stamps	£4.55
20 April	Window cleaning	£12.00
25 April	Donation to charity	£10.00

At 30 April the petty cash remaining in the locked box comprised:

1 x £10 note, 7 x £5 notes, 5 x £1 coins, 1 x 50p coin, 1 x 20p coin, 1 x 10p coin, 2 x 5p coins, 1 x 2p coin, 3 x 1p coins

solution

- Total payments for April are £49.05
- Therefore cash remaining should be £100.00 – £49.05 = £50.95

• Actual cash remaining is:

	as at 30 April	
	number held	value (£)
£10 notes	1	10.00
£5 notes	7	35.00
£1 coins	5	5.00
50p coins	1	0.50
20p coins	1	0.20
10p coins	1	0.10
5p coins	2	0.10
2p coins	1	0.02
1p coins	3	0.03
TOTAL		50.95

• Therefore, at 30 April, the petty cash book reconciles (agrees) with cash in hand

Notes on the Case Study:

• If there is a discrepancy, it should be investigated promptly and, if it cannot be resolved should be referred to the accounts supervisor.

• From a practical point of view it is advisable to keep the cash in the form of lower denomination notes and a stock of coins – these will make it easier to pay out the amounts of petty cash claims (with less risk of error) than if larger denomination notes, such as £50 and £20, are used.

HOW PETTY CASH BOOK FITS INTO THE ACCOUNTING SYSTEM

In the accounting system the petty cash book may combine the roles of the book of prime entry and double-entry book-keeping. This means that the petty cash book is:

• the book of prime entry for low value expense payments

• the double-entry account for petty cash (kept in general ledger)

The diagram on the next page shows petty cash book performing both of these functions within the accounting system. The diagram shows the flow involving:

- financial documents – petty cash vouchers
- the petty cash book as a book of prime entry
- double-entry book-keeping, involving petty cash and the other ledgers

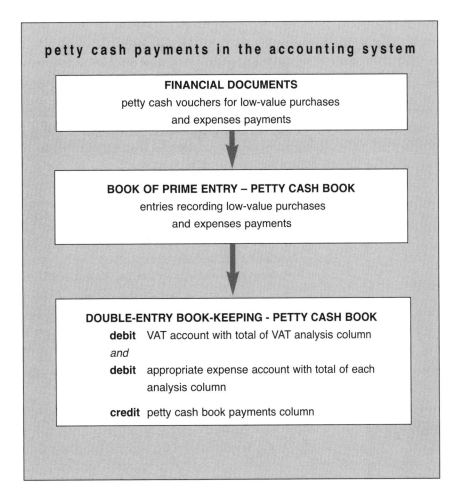

the use of petty cash control account

In some accounting systems the petty cash book is used only as a book of prime entry; in such circumstances, a general ledger account called petty cash control account is used in the accounting system to complete double-entry.

To illustrate the use of petty cash control account we will use Wyvern Traders' petty cash book (on page 127). The totals of receipts and payments are entered in petty cash control account (which has been given the account number GL0180) as follows:

GENERAL LEDGER

Dr			Petty Cash Control Account (GL0180)		Cr
20-4		£	20-4		£
5 Apr	Balance b/d	100.00	9 Apr	Petty cash book PCB30	61.20
9 Apr	Bank CB55	61.20	9 Apr	Balance c/d	100.00
		161.20			161.20
10 Apr	Balance b/d	100.00			

Notes:

- The debit 'Balance b/d' on 5 April of £100.00 is the same as the opening balance in petty cash book – see page 127. This is the imprest amount for this petty cash book.

- The credit entry for 'Petty cash book PCB30' on 9 April of £61.20 is the total of the analysis columns (VAT and expenses) from petty cash book. These amounts are debited to their respective accounts in general ledger.

- The debit entry for 'Bank CB55' on 9 April for £61.20 is the reimbursement of petty cash in order to restore the imprest amount. The cheque requisition for this is shown on page 128.

- The 'Balance c/d' on 9 April (and brought down on 10 April) for £100.00 is the new balance on petty cash book, ready for next week's transactions.

- In petty cash control account, the cross reference to petty cash book enables a transaction to be followed through the accounting system – from book of prime entry to double-entry account – to ensure that it is complete.

Chapter Summary

- The purpose of the petty cash book is to record low-value cash payments for small purchases and expenses incurred by a business.

- The person responsible for maintaining the petty cash book is the petty cashier, who is responsible for security.

- Payment can only be made from the petty cash book against correct documentation – usually a petty cash voucher, which must be signed by the person authorising payment.

- Where a business is registered for Value Added Tax, it must record VAT amounts paid on petty cash purchases in a separate column in the petty cash book.

- At regular intervals – weekly or monthly – the petty cash book is balanced; the total of each analysis column is debited to the relevant account in the general ledger, and the petty cashier will restore the imprest amount of cash.

- Petty cash book may combine the roles of:
  - the book of prime entry for low-value cash payments
  - the double-entry account for petty cash

- When petty cash book is used only as a book of prime entry, a petty cash control account is used in general ledger to complete double-entry book-keeping.

Key Terms		
petty cash book		records low-value cash payments for small purchases and expenses; may combine the roles of the book of prime entry for low-value cash payments and the double-entry account for petty cash
petty cashier		person responsible for the petty cash book
petty cash voucher		financial document against which payments are made out of petty cash
imprest system		where the money held in the petty cash float is restored to the same amount for the beginning of each week or month
petty cash float		amount of money received by the petty cashier from the firm's cashier at the beginning of the period to be used for petty cash payments
analysis columns		used in petty cash book to record expense payments under various headings to suit the circumstances of the business
petty cash control account		double-entry account in general ledger used when petty cash book is treated solely as the book of prime entry; it shows the total payments made by the petty cashier during the week or month, and records receipts from bank account together with the opening and closing balances

Activities

7.1 Most petty cash books operate using the imprest system. This means that:

(a) the petty cashier draws money from the cashier as and when required

(b) the cashier has to authorise each petty cash payment

(c) a copy has to be kept of each petty cash voucher

(d) the petty cashier starts each week or month with a fixed amount of money

Which one of these options is correct?

7.2 You are employed as an accounts assistant for Temeside Printers Limited. As a training exercise the accounts supervisor asks you which of the following expenses you would allow to be paid out of petty cash? The upper limit for petty cash transactions is £30.

(a) postage on a parcel of printing sent to a customer, £5.50

(b) a rubber date stamp bought for use in the office, £10.30

(c) rail fare to work claimed by the office manager's secretary, £6.50

(d) donation to charity, £10.00

(e) tea and coffee for use by office staff, £8.00

(f) mileage allowance claimed by works foreman who had to visit a customer, £15.45

(g) meal allowance paid to assistant who had to work her lunch hour, £5.00

(h) window cleaning, £7.00

(i) purchase of shelving for the office, £65.00

(j) taxi fare claimed for delivering an urgent parcel of printing to a customer, £16.50

Note: you may assume that all expenses are supported by relevant documentation.

Explain any expenses that you will refer to the accounts supervisor.

7.3 As petty cashier, prepare petty cash vouchers under today's date for signature by the person making the claim. You are able to authorise payments up to £10.00 each. A blank voucher is shown below. Alternatively you can download blank documents from www.osbornebooks.co.uk

- £4.45 claimed by Jayne Smith for postage (no VAT) on a recorded delivery letter sent to a customer, Evelode Supplies Limited.
- £2.35, including VAT, claimed by Tanya Howard for air mail envelopes bought for use in the office.
- £8.60, including VAT, claimed by Toni Wyatt for a taxi fare used on a business visit to a customer, Jasper Limited.

Number the vouchers, beginning with number 851

What documentation will you require to be attached to each voucher?

petty cash voucher		number		
		date		
description			amount	
			£	p
VAT at 17.5%				
signature	....			
authorised	....			

7.4 The business for which you work is registered for VAT. The following petty cash amounts include VAT at 17.5% and you are required to calculate the amount that will be shown in the VAT column and the appropriate expense column (remember that VAT amounts should be rounded down to the nearest penny):

(a) £9.40
(b) £4.70
(c) £2.35
(d) £2.45
(e) £5.60
(f) £3.47
(g) £8.75
(h) 94p
(i) 99p
(j) £9.41

7.5   The petty cashier of the company where you work as an accounts assistant is away on holiday. The accounts supervisor asks you to balance the petty cash book at 31 August. The petty cash book uses the imprest system and the imprest amount is £100.00.

You are to:

- restore the imprest amount of petty cash to £100.00, making appropriate entries in the petty cash book

- balance the petty cash book at 31 August 20-2 and bring down the balances on 1 September

Receipts	Date	Details	Voucher number	Total payment	Analysis columns				
					VAT	Postages	Travel	Meals	Office sundries
£	20-2			£	£	£	£	£	£
100.00	1 Aug	Balance b/d							
	4 Aug	Postages	323	10.20		10.20			
	6 Aug	Travel expenses	324	8.50			8.50		
	9 Aug	Postages	325	5.60		5.60			
	12 Aug	Envelopes	326	9.40	1.40				800
	13 Aug	Window cleaning	327	14.10	2.10				12.00
	17 Aug	Taxi fare	328	11.75	1.75		10.00		
	20 Aug	Postages	329	9.40		9.40			
	23 Aug	Meals	330	12.20				12.20	
	27 Aug	Envelopes	331	7.52	1.12				6.40

Petty Cash Book   PCB55

7.6   On returning from holiday, you are told to take charge of the petty cash book of Carr Trading. This is kept using the imprest system, the float being £150.00 at the beginning of each month. Analysis columns are used for VAT, travel, postages, stationery, meals, and miscellaneous.

There are a number of transactions for the month which have been authorised. All transactions, unless otherwise indicated, include VAT at 17.5%.

20-3

1 Aug   Balance of cash £150.00

4 Aug   Voucher no 39: taxi fare £9.40

6 Aug   Voucher no 40: postage £5.50 (no VAT)

9 Aug	Voucher no 41: marker pens £3.76
11 Aug	Voucher no 42: travel expenses £10.50 (no VAT)
12 Aug	Voucher no 43: window cleaner £14.10
16 Aug	Voucher no 44: large envelopes £4.70
18 Aug	Voucher no 45: donation to charity £10.00 (no VAT)
19 Aug	Voucher no 46: rail fare £10.60 (no VAT); meal allowance £6.00 (no VAT)
20 Aug	Voucher no 47: recorded delivery postage £2.30 (no VAT)
23 Aug	Voucher no 48: roll of packing tape £2.35
25 Aug	Voucher no 49: excess postage paid £1.50 (no VAT)
27 Aug	Voucher no 50: taxi fare £14.10

You are to:

- Enter the transactions for the month on page 42 of the petty cash book.
- Total the analysis columns.
- Restore the imprest amount of petty cash book to £150.00 by transfer from the cash book.
- Balance the petty cash book at 31 August 20-3 and bring down the balance on 1 September.

7.7 Towan Limited keeps an amount of petty cash in a locked box in the office. The imprest amount is £150 which is restored at the beginning of each month.

The following payments were made in June and have been recorded in the petty cash book:

3 June	Postage stamps	£5.85
7 June	Window cleaning	£12.50
10 June	Stationery	£7.25
15 June	Meal allowance	£8.00
18 June	Donation to charity	£10.00
20 June	Stationery	£9.47
24 June	Postage stamps	£3.65

At 30 June the petty cash remaining in the locked box comprised:

3 x £10 notes, 8 x £5 notes, 15 x £1 coins, 11 x 50p coins, 6 x 20p coins, 11 x 10p coins, 5 x 5p coins, 6 x 2p coins, 11 x 1p coins

You are to complete the following:

(a)

Total of petty cash payments for June	£
Cash remaining should be	£

Actual cash remaining is:

	as at 30 June	
	number held	value (£)
£10 notes		
£5 notes		
£1 coins		
50p coins		
20p coins		
10p coins		
5p coins		
2p coins		
1p coins		
TOTAL		
Amount of discrepancy (if any)		£

(b)   State what action should be taken when a petty cash book cannot be reconciled with cash in hand.

7.8 Prepare the petty cash book for Syston Systems Limited. This is kept solely as a book of prime entry. It uses the imprest system, the float being £150.00.

Analysis columns are used for VAT, postages, travel, meals, and sundry office expenses.

20-4

7 June	Balance of cash £150.00
7 June	Postages £6.35 (no VAT), voucher no 123
8 June	Travel expenses £8.25 (no VAT), voucher no 124
8 June	Postages £3.28 (no VAT), voucher no 125
9 June	Envelopes £4.70, voucher no 126
9 June	Window cleaning £14.10, voucher no 127
10 June	Taxi fare £7.05, meal £14.10, voucher no 128
10 June	Postages £8.50 (no VAT), packing materials £5.64, voucher no 129
10 June	Taxi fare £14.10, meal £9.40, voucher no 130
11 June	Marker pens £2.52, envelopes £5.00, voucher no 131

You are to:

(a) Enter the above authorised transactions for the week on page 18 of the petty cash book. The voucher amounts include VAT at 17.5% unless indicated.

Total the analysis columns and restore the imprest amount of petty cash book to £150.00 by transfer from the cash book.

(b) Balance the petty cash book as at 11 June 20-4 and bring down the balance on 12 June.

(c) Show how the petty cash control account is written up in the general ledger of Syston Systems Limited.

8 Using control accounts

this chapter covers...

In this chapter we look at control accounts which are used as 'master' accounts to control a number of memorandum accounts.

A control account (also known as a totals account) is used to record the total of transactions passing through the memorandum accounts. In this way, the balance of the control account will always be equal (unless an error has occurred) to the total balances of the memorandum accounts.

The three control accounts we will study in this chapter are:

- *sales ledger control account – the total of receivables (also known as debtors)*

- *purchases ledger control account – the total of payables (also known as creditors)*

- *Value Added Tax control account – the total of VAT due to or from HM Revenue & Customs*

The chapter explains:

- *the purpose of control accounts*

- *how control accounts work*

- *reconciling control accounts to memorandum accounts*

- *the layout of control accounts*

- *how control accounts fit into the accounting system*

- *information sources for control accounts*

THE PURPOSE OF CONTROL ACCOUNTS

Control accounts are 'master' accounts which control a number of subsidiary 'memorandum' accounts, – individual supplier or customer accounts, for example. This set-up can be illustrated as follows:

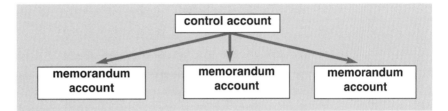

The control account (also known as a **totals account**) is used to record the totals of transactions passing through the memorandum accounts. In this way, the balance of the control account will always be equal to the total balances of the memorandum accounts, unless an error has occurred.

Three commonly-used control accounts in an accounting system are:

- **sales ledger control account**, which controls the sales ledger

- **purchases ledger control account**, which controls the purchases ledger

- **Value Added Tax control account**, which brings together totals of VAT from books of prime entry, such as the day books and cash book

Note: each of these control accounts is a general ledger account in the accounting system.

In the illustration above we have seen how a control account acts as a master account for a number of memorandum accounts. The principle is that, if the total of the opening balances for memorandum accounts is known, together with the total of amounts increasing these balances, and the total of amounts decreasing these balances, then the total of the closing balances for the memorandum accounts can be calculated.

For example:

	£
Total of opening balances	50,000
Add increases	10,000
	60,000
Less decreases	12,000
Total of closing balances	48,000

The total of the closing balances can now be reconciled (agreed) against a separate listing of the balances of the memorandum accounts to ensure that the two figures agree. If they do, it proves that the ledgers within the section are correct, unless an error has occurred within the ledger section.

SALES LEDGER CONTROL ACCOUNT

how sales ledger control account works

The diagram on the next page shows the personal memorandum accounts which form the sales ledger of a particular business – in practice there would be more than four accounts involved. The sales ledger control account acts as a totals account, which records totals of the transactions passing through the accounts which it controls. Note that transactions are shown in the control account **on the same side** as in the memorandum accounts.

Sales ledger control account is reconciled with the balances of the memorandum accounts which it controls. Thus, control accounts act as an aid to locating errors: if the control account and memorandum accounts agree, then the error is likely to lie elsewhere. In this way the control account acts as an intermediate checking device – proving the arithmetical accuracy of the ledger section unless an error has occurred within the ledger section.

reconciling sales ledger control account

At regular intervals – eg weekly or monthly – a business reconciles the balances of memorandum accounts in sales ledger with the balance of sales ledger control account. To carry out this reconciliation, the balances of the memorandum accounts in sales ledger are listed and then totalled – the total should agree with the balance of sales ledger control account. Any discrepancy (see page 151) should be investigated immediately and the error(s) traced.

Using the accounts shown on the next page the sales ledger control account and the memorandum sales ledger accounts will be agreed at the beginning and end of the month, as follows:

Reconciliation of sales ledger control account		
	1 January 20-4	*31 January 20-4*
	£	£
A Ackroyd	100	150
B Barnes	200	200
C Cox	50	180
D Douglas	150	150
Sales ledger control account	500	680

GENERAL LEDGER

Dr		Sales Ledger Control Account			Cr
20-4			£	20-4	£
1 Jan	Balance b/d	500		31 Jan Bank	443
31 Jan	Sales	700		31 Jan Discount allowed	7
				31 Jan Sales returns	70
				31 Jan Balance c/d	680
		1,200			1,200
1 Feb	Balance b/d	680			

SALES LEDGER

Dr		A Ackroyd			Cr
20-4			£	20-4	£
1 Jan	Balance b/d	100		12 Jan Bank	98
6 Jan	Sales	150		12 Jan Discount allowed	2
				31 Jan Balance c/d	150
		250			250
1 Feb	Balance b/d	150			

Dr		B Barnes			Cr
20-4			£	20-4	£
1 Jan	Balance b/d	200		13 Jan Bank	195
6 Jan	Sales	250		13 Jan Discount allowed	5
				27 Jan Sales returns	50
				31 Jan Balance c/d	200
		450			450
1 Feb	Balance b/d	200			

Dr		C Cox			Cr
20-4			£	20-4	£
1 Jan	Balance b/d	50		20 Jan Bank	50
15 Jan	Sales	200		29 Jan Sales returns	20
				31 Jan Balance c/d	180
		250			250
1 Feb	Balance b/d	180			

Dr		D Douglas			Cr
20-4			£	20-4	£
1 Jan	Balance b/d	150		30 Jan Bank	100
20 Jan	Sales	100		31 Jan Balance c/d	150
		250			250
1 Feb	Balance b/d	150			

sales ledger control account explained

The layout of the sales ledger control account is shown below, with sample figures.

Study the layout carefully and then read the text which follows:

Dr		Sales Ledger Control Account		Cr
	£			£
Balance b/d	2,900	Cash/cheques received from customers		12,100
Credit sales	14,000	Settlement (cash) discount allowed		290
Returned cheques	520	Sales returns		870
Interest charged to customers	410	Bad debts written off		1,590
		Set-off/contra entries		250
		Balance c/d		2,730
	17,830			17,830
Balance b/d	2,730			

balance b/d

The figure for balance b/d on the debit side of the control account represents the total of the balances of the individual customer accounts in the sales ledger. This principle has been seen in the diagram on page 145. Remember that, at the end of the month (or other period covered by the control account), the account must be balanced and carried down (on the credit side) on the last day of the month, and then brought down (on the debit side) on the first day of the next month.

Note that it is possible for a customer's account to have a credit balance, instead of the usual debit balance. This may come about, for example, because the customer has paid for goods and then returned them, or has overpaid in error: the business owes the amount due, ie the customer has a credit balance for the time being. Most accounting systems 'net off' any such credit balances against the debit balances to give an overall figure for receivables (debtors).

credit sales

Only credit sales – and not cash sales – are entered in the control account because only credit sales are recorded in the customers' accounts. However, the total sales of a business may well comprise both credit and cash sales.

dishonoured cheques

If a customer's cheque is dishonoured – returned unpaid – by the bank, ie the cheque has 'bounced', then authorisation for the entries to be made in the accounting system must be given by the accounts supervisor. These entries are:

– *debit* sales ledger control account

– *credit* cash book (bank columns)

The transaction must also be recorded in the customer's account in the sales ledger – on the debit side.

Note that the returned cheque is the prime document for the adjustment – like other prime documents it should be stored securely for future reference.

Dishonoured cheques have been discussed earlier on page 89.

bad debts written off

A bad debt is a debt owing to a business which it considers will never be paid.

We will look in more detail at bad debts written off in the next chapter. For the moment the accounting entries after a bad debt has been authorised for write off are:

– *debit* bad debts account

– *credit* sales ledger control account

The transaction must also be recorded in the customer's account in sales ledger – on the credit side.

set-off/contra entries

These entries occur when the same person or business has a memorandum account in both the sales ledger and the purchases ledger, ie they are both buying from, and selling to, the business whose accounts we are preparing.

Set-off contra entries are looked at in more detail on page158, where we will see the entries which affect the control accounts.

sales ledger control account in the accounting system

The diagram on the next page shows how sales ledger control account is incorporated in general ledger of the accounting system, with the customers' accounts kept as memorandum accounts in sales ledger.

- **Sales ledger control account is part of the double-entry system**
- **Customer accounts are in sales ledger as memorandum accounts**

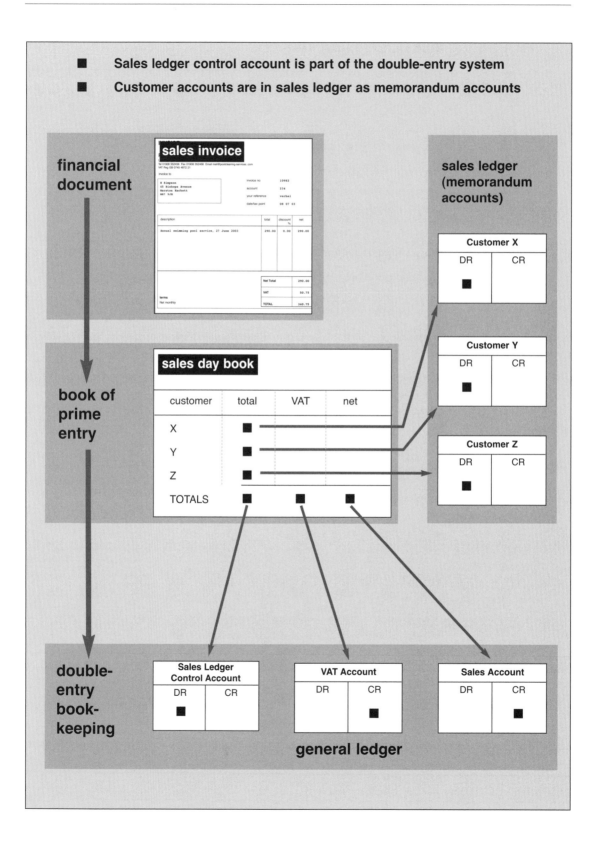

From time-to-time, the balances of the sales ledger memorandum accounts are reconciled with the balance of sales ledger control account, and any discrepancies investigated.

information sources for sales ledger control account

Control accounts use totals (remember that their other name is 'totals accounts') for the week, month, quarter or year – depending on what time period is decided upon by the business. The totals for sales ledger control account come from a number of sources in the accounting system:

- total credit sales (including VAT) – from the 'total' column of the sales day book
- total sales returns (including VAT) – from the 'total' column of the sales returns day book
- total cash/cheques received from customers – from the cash book (see Chapter 5)
- total settlement discount allowed – from the discount allowed column of the cash book (see Chapter 5), or from discount allowed account
- bad debts – from the journal, or bad debts written off account (see Chapter 9)

using an aged debtor analysis

An **aged debtor analysis** is a summary of each receivable (debtor) balance from sales ledger analysed into columns showing how long the amounts have been outstanding. It is used by a business to show which customers are slow in paying and enables the business to decide which customers to chase for payment.

An example of an aged debtor analysis is given below.

Wyvern Trading Aged debtor analysis at 30 September 20-6				
Customer	Total	0-30 days	31-60 days	61+ days
	£	£	£	£
Adams Ltd	3,510	0	0	3,510
T Brewster	1,840	1,620	220	0
Harrison & Co	760	760	0	0
D Miller	2,330	330	2,000	0
Totals	8,440	2,710	2,220	3,510

An aged debtor analysis can either be drawn up manually, or it can be printed out from a computer accounting package.

The analysis is normally produced at the end of each month when statements are sent out to customers. From the analysis (see previous page) the business decides which customers it is going to chase up, and how. It may send a letter, an email, or it may telephone the customer. For example, from the above aged debtor analysis, the account of Adams Ltd is overdue for payment and a strongly worded letter, followed up with a telephone call might be needed; most of the balance of D Miller's account is now overdue and a letter or email might be sent as a reminder; the account of T Brewster is partly overdue but it is unlikely that any action will be taken this month; the account of Harrison & Co is 'in order'.

dealing with discrepancies

As stated earlier, it is important at regular intervals to reconcile the balances of memorandum accounts in sales ledger with the balance of sales ledger control account. The diagram on the opposite page shows where error(s) might occur. The first thing to do is to establish:

- is the balance of sales ledger control account greater than the total of the balances of the memorandum accounts in sales ledger?

  or

- is the total of the balances of the memorandum accounts in sales ledger greater than the balance of sales ledger control account?

Once this has been established, the relevant column from the diagram indicates what may have caused the discrepancy. The discrepancy can then be investigated, the error(s) traced and any problems solved.

PURCHASES LEDGER CONTROL ACCOUNT

how purchases ledger control account works

The diagram on page 152 shows the personal accounts which form the purchases ledger of a particular business – in practice there would be more than four accounts involved.

Purchases ledger control account acts as a totals account, which records totals of the transactions passing through the memorandum accounts which it controls. Note that transactions are shown in the control account on the same side as in the memorandum accounts.

continued on page 153

Discrepancies between sales ledger control account (slca) and sales ledger (sl)		
possible discrepancy	slca greater than sl	sl greater than slca
credit sales		
– omitted/understated in slca	✗	✔
– omitted/understated in sl	✔	✗
– entered twice/overstated in slca	✔	✗
– entered twice/overstated in sl	✗	✔
sales returns		
– omitted/understated in slca	✔	✗
– omitted/understated in sl	✗	✔
– entered twice/overstated in slca	✗	✔
– entered twice/overstated in sl	✔	✗
money received from receivables (debtors)		
– omitted/understated in slca	✔	✗
– omitted/understated in sl	✗	✔
– entered twice/overstated in slca	✗	✔
– entered twice/overstated in sl	✔	✗
settlement (cash) discount		
– omitted/understated in slca	✔	✗
– omitted/understated in sl	✗	✔
– entered twice/overstated in slca	✗	✔
– entered twice/overstated in sl	✔	✗
bad debts written off		
– omitted/understated in slca	✔	✗
– omitted/understated in sl	✗	✔
– entered twice/overstated in slca	✗	✔
– entered twice/overstated in sl	✔	✗
other		
– debit balance recorded in error as credit in sl	✔	✗
– credit balance recorded in error as debit in sl	✗	✔

GENERAL LEDGER

Dr	Purchases Ledger Control Account		Cr	
20-4		£	20-4	£
31 Jan	Purchases returns	150	1 Jan Balance b/d	1,000
31 Jan	Bank	594	31 Jan Purchases	1,700
31 Jan	Discount received	6		
31 Jan	Balance c/d	1,950		
		2,700		2,700
			1 Feb Balance b/d	1,950

PURCHASES LEDGER

Dr	F Francis		Cr	
20-4		£	20-4	£
16 Jan	Bank	98	1 Jan Balance b/d	100
16 Jan	Discount received	2	2 Jan Purchases	200
31 Jan	Balance c/d	200		
		300		300
			1 Feb Balance b/d	200

Dr	G Gold		Cr	
20-4		£	20-4	£
15 Jan	Purchases returns	50	1 Jan Balance b/d	200
28 Jan	Bank	100	9 Jan Purchases	300
31 Jan	Balance c/d	350		
		500		500
			1 Feb Balance b/d	350

Dr	H Harris		Cr	
20-4		£	20-4	£
28 Jan	Purchases returns	100	1 Jan Balance b/d	300
30 Jan	Bank	200	16 Jan Purchases	500
31 Jan	Balance c/d	500		
		800		800
			1 Feb Balance b/d	500

Dr	I Ingram		Cr	
20-4		£	20-4	£
22 Jan	Bank	196	1 Jan Balance b/d	400
22 Jan	Discount received	4	27 Jan Purchases	700
31 Jan	Balance c/d	900		
		1,100		1,100
			1 Feb Balance b/d	900

reconciling purchases ledger control account

At regular intervals – eg weekly or monthly – a business reconciles the balances of memorandum accounts in purchases ledger with the balances of sales ledger control account. To carry out this reconciliation, the balances of the memorandum accounts in purchases ledger are listed and then totalled – the total should agree with the balance of purchases ledger control account. Any discrepancy should be investigated immediately and the error(s) traced.

From the diagram on the previous page the purchases ledger control account and the memorandum purchases ledger accounts will be agreed at the beginning and end of the month, as follows:

Reconciliation of purchases ledger control account		
	1 January 20-4	*31 January 20-4*
	£	£
F Francis	100	200
G Gold	200	350
H Harris	300	500
I Ingram	400	900
Purchases ledger control account	1,000	1,950

purchases ledger control account explained

The layout of the purchases ledger control account is shown below, with sample figures.

Study the layout carefully and then read the text on the next page.

Dr		Purchases Ledger Control Account		Cr
	£			£
Cash/cheques paid to suppliers	8,200	Balance b/d		5,000
Settlement (cash) discount received	260	Credit purchases		8,500
Purchases returns	1,070			
Set-off/contra entries	120			
Balance c/d	3,850			
	13,500			13,500
		Balance b/d		3,850

balance b/d

The figure for balance b/d on the credit side of the control account represents the total of the balances of the individual payables' (creditors') accounts in the purchases ledger. This principle has been seen in the diagram on the page 152.

Note that it is possible for a supplier's account to have a debit balance, instead of the usual credit balance. This may come about, for example, if the supplier has been overpaid. Most accounting systems 'net off' any such debit balances against the credit balances to give an overall figure for suppliers.

credit purchases

Only credit purchases – and not cash purchases – are entered in the control account because only credit purchases are recorded in the suppliers' accounts. However, the total purchases of a business may well comprise both credit and cash purchases.

set-off/contra entries

These entries occur when the same person or business has a memorandum account in both the purchases ledger and the sales ledger, ie they are both selling to, and buying from, the business whose accounts we are preparing.

Set-off/contra entries are looked at in more detail in the next section, where we will see the entries which affect the control accounts.

purchases ledger control account in the accounting system

The diagram on the next page shows how purchases ledger control account is incorporated in the general ledger of the accounting system, with the suppliers' accounts kept as memorandum accounts in the purchases ledger.

From time-to-time, the balances of the purchases ledger memorandum accounts are agreed with the balance of purchases ledger control account, and any discrepancies investigated.

- **Purchases ledger control account is part of the double-entry system**
- **Suppliers' accounts are in purchases ledger as memorandum accounts**

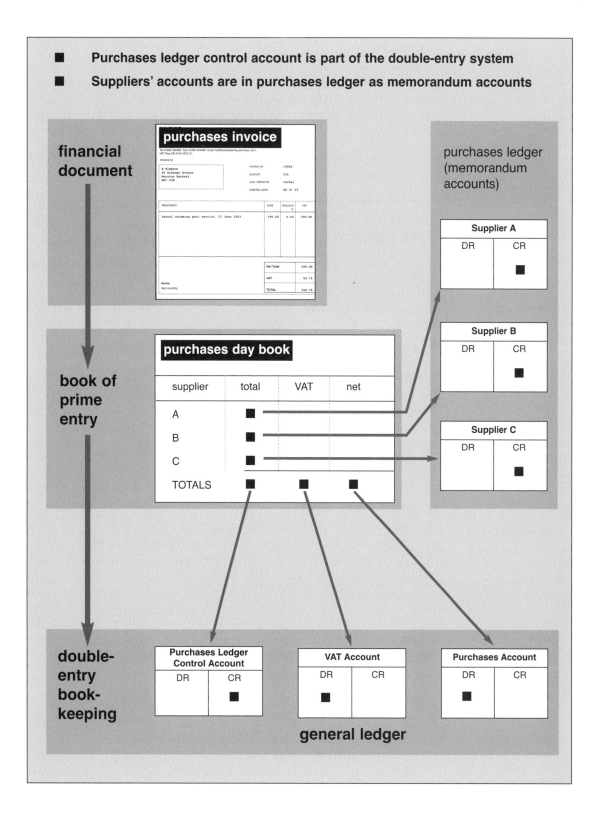

financial
document

purchases ledger
(memorandum
accounts)

book of
prime
entry

double-
entry
book-
keeping

general ledger

information sources for purchases ledger control account

Control accounts use totals (remember that their other name is totals accounts) for the week, month, quarter or year – depending on what time period is decided upon by the business. The totals for purchases ledger control account come from a number of sources in the accounting system:

- total credit purchases (including VAT) – from the 'total' column of the purchases day book

- total purchases returns (including VAT) – from the 'total' column of the purchases returns day book

- total cash/cheques paid to suppliers – from the cash book (see Chapter 5)

- total settlement discount received – from the discount received column of the cash book (see Chapter 5), or from discount received account

using an aged creditor analysis

An **aged creditor analysis** works in the same way as an aged debtor analysis (see page 149), except that it is a summary of each payable (creditor) balance. It is used by a business to show how long accounts have been outstanding and it enables the business to decide which suppliers to pay.

dealing with discrepancies

As we have seen earlier, it is important to reconcile the balances of memorandum accounts in purchases ledger with the balance of purchases ledger control account. The diagram on the next page shows where error(s) might occur. The first thing to do is to establish:

- is the balance of purchases ledger control account greater than the total of the balances of the memorandum accounts in purchases ledger?

  or

- is the total of the balances of the memorandum accounts in purchases ledger greater than the balance of purchases ledger control account?

Once this has been established, the relevant column from the diagram indicates what may have caused the discrepancy. The discrepancy can then be investigated, the error(s) traced and any problems solved.

Discrepancies between purchases ledger control account (plca) and purchases ledger (pl)		
possible discrepancy	plca greater than pl	pl greater than plca
credit purchases		
– omitted/understated in plca	✗	✔
– omitted/understated in pl	✔	✗
– entered twice/overstated in plca	✔	✗
– entered twice/overstated in pl	✗	✔
purchases returns		
– omitted/understated in plca	✔	✗
– omitted/understated in pl	✗	✔
– entered twice/overstated in plca	✗	✔
– entered twice/overstated in pl	✔	✗
money paid to payables (creditors)		
– omitted/understated in plca	✔	✗
– omitted/understated in pl	✗	✔
– entered twice/overstated in plca	✗	✔
– entered twice/overstated in pl	✔	✗
settlement (cash) discount		
– omitted/understated in plca	✔	✗
– omitted/understated in pl	✗	✔
– entered twice/overstated in plca	✗	✔
– entered twice/overstated in pl	✔	✗
other		
– credit balance recorded in error as debit in pl	✔	✗
– debit balance recorded in error as credit in pl	✗	✔

SET-OFF/CONTRA ENTRIES

These entries occur when the same person or business has a memorandum account in both subsidiary ledgers – sales ledger and purchases ledger – ie they are both buying from, and selling to, the business whose accounts we are preparing. For example, Patel Limited has the following accounts in the sales and purchases ledgers:

SALES LEDGER

Dr		A Smith		Cr
		£		£
Balance b/d		200		

PURCHASES LEDGER

Dr		A Smith		Cr
		£		£
			Balance b/d	300

From these accounts we can see that:

- A Smith owes Patel Limited £200 (sales ledger)
- Patel Limited owes A Smith £300 (purchases ledger)

To save each having to make a bank payment to the other, it is possible (with A Smith's agreement) to set-off one account against the other, so that they can settle their net indebtedness with one bank payment. The book-keeping entries in Patel's books will be:

– *debit* A Smith (purchases ledger) £200

– *credit* A Smith (sales ledger) £200

The accounts will now appear as:

SALES LEDGER

Dr		A Smith		Cr
		£		£
Balance b/d		200	Set-off: purchases ledger	200

PURCHASES LEDGER

Dr		A Smith		Cr
	£			£
Set-off: sales ledger	200	Balance b/d		300

The net result is that Patel Limited owes A Smith £100. The important point to note is that, because transactions have been recorded in the subsidiary ledger accounts, an entry needs to be made in the two control accounts:

– *debit* purchases ledger control account

– *credit* sales ledger control account

Set-off transactions should be appropriately documented and authorised.

VALUE ADDED TAX (VAT) CONTROL ACCOUNT

how VAT control account works

VAT control account brings together totals of VAT from books of prime entry, such as the day books and cash book. The diagram on page 161 shows how VAT control account fits into the accounting system.

It is from VAT control account that the VAT Return is prepared, checked and then submitted, normally online, to HM Revenue and Customs – often quarterly, ie every three months. VAT return shows:

- either, the money amount due to be paid by the business when VAT collected from sales is greater than the VAT paid on purchases
- or, the money amount due as a refund from HM Revenue & Customs to the business when VAT collected from sales is less than the VAT paid on purchases

reconciling VAT control account

Whilst VAT control account does not have memorandum accounts in sales or purchases ledger to reconcile against, it is nevertheless a totals account. The VAT amounts must be recorded from the books of prime entry; the balance of VAT control account tells the business how much is due to or from HM Revenue & Customs. The account balance must reconcile with the amount shown on the business VAT return – any discrepancy should be investigated immediately and the error(s) traced.

VAT control account explained

A typical layout of a VAT control account with sample figures is shown below. Study the layout carefully and then read the text which follows.

Dr		VAT Control Account		Cr
	£			£
Purchases	30,000	Sales		40,000
Sales returns	1,500	Purchases returns		1,000
Cash purchases	4,000	Cash sales		5,000
Other cash expenses	700	Other cash income		300
Balance c/d	10,100			
	46,300			46,300
		Balance b/d		10,100

purchases

This the the amount of VAT taken from the totals row of purchases day book, which is the VAT paid by the business on its credit purchases.

sales returns

Here is recorded the amount of VAT taken from the totals row of sales returns day book. This is the VAT allowed back to customers of the business on the sales returns they make.

cash purchases and other cash expenses

The total of the VAT column from the payments side of cash book is debited to VAT control account. This total will comprise VAT paid on the cash purchases of the business, including other expenses – both capital and revenue – paid for as cash transactions.

sales

This is the amount of VAT taken from the totals row of sales day book, which is the VAT calculated by the business on its credit sales.

purchases returns

Here is recorded the amount of VAT taken from the totals row of purchases returns day book. This is the VAT allowed back to the business by its suppliers on purchases returns.

continued on page 162

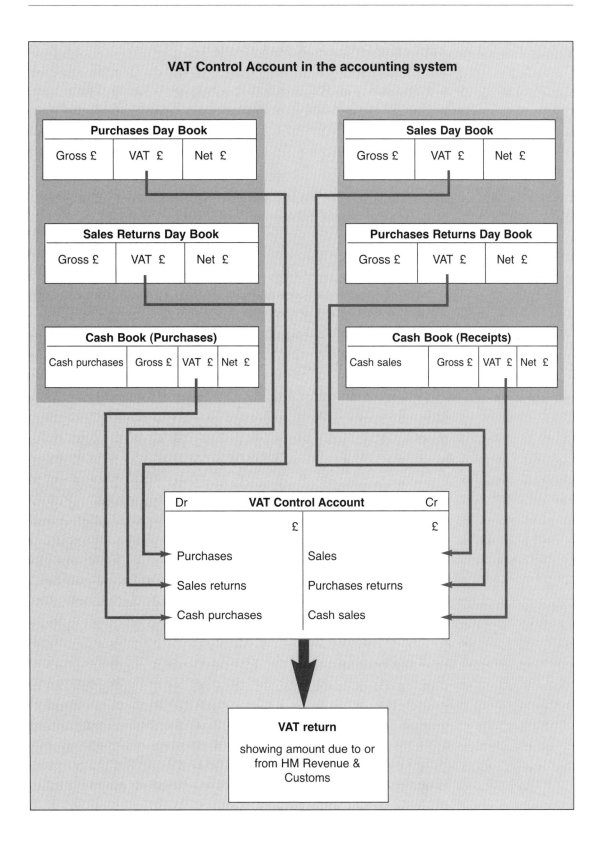

cash sales and other cash income

The total of the VAT column from the receipts side of cash book is credited to VAT control account. This total will comprise VAT collected on the cash sales of the business, including other income – both capital and revenue – received as cash transactions.

the journal

Another book of prime entry is the journal – which is discussed in detail in the next chapter. From time-to-time there may be an entry from the journal to VAT control account – however this will be for a non-regular transaction.

balance

The balance on VAT control account can be either debit or credit:

- a debit balance brought down indicates that the amount is due as a refund to the business from HM Revenue & Customs

- a credit balance brought down indicates that the amount is due to be paid by the business to HM Revenue & Customs (which is the situation for the majority of businesses)

The balance of the account will be settled with a bank payment either from or to HM Revenue & Customs.

VAT control account in the accounting system

VAT control account is a general ledger account which uses totals from the books of prime entry, including cash book. The account is the source information for preparation of the VAT return of the business, which is submitted to HM Revenue & Customs. The balance of VAT control account must reconcile with (agree with) the VAT Return.

CONTROL ACCOUNTS AS AN AID TO MANAGEMENT

instant information

When the manager of a business needs to know the figure for receivables or payables or VAT – important information for the manager – the balance of the appropriate control account will give the information immediately. There is no need to add up the balances of all the memorandum customer/supplier accounts, or to go to the books of prime entry for VAT amounts.

With a computer accounting system, the control accounts can be printed at any time.

prevention of fraud

The use of control accounts makes fraud more difficult – particularly in a manual accounting system. If a fraudulent transaction is to be recorded on a memorandum account, the transaction must also be entered in the control account. As the control account will be either maintained by a supervisor, or checked regularly by the manager, the control accounts add another level of security within the accounting system. In most accounting systems, staff are only able to access the accounting information appropriate to their work.

location of errors

Control accounts can also help in locating errors. Remember, though, that a control account only proves the arithmetical accuracy of the accounts which it controls – there could still be errors within the subsidiary ledger section.

limitation of control accounts

Whilst control accounts can help in locating errors, they do have the limitation that not all errors will be shown. For example, if a transaction is entered into the wrong debtor's memorandum account within sales ledger, this will not be revealed when the control account is reconciled to the memorandum accounts.

Chapter Summary

■ Control accounts (or totals accounts) are 'master' accounts, which control a number of memorandum accounts.

■ Three commonly used control accounts are:
   – sales ledger control account
   – purchases ledger control account
   – Value Added Tax control account

■ Transactions are recorded on the same side of the control account as on the memorandum accounts.

■ Set-off/contra entries occur when one person has a memorandum account in both subsidiary ledgers – sales ledger and purchases ledger – and it is agreed to set-off one balance against the other to leave a net balance. This usually results in the following control account entries:
   – *debit* purchases ledger control account
   – *credit* sales ledger control account

■ In most accounting systems, control accounts are incorporated into the general ledger of the double-entry book-keeping system. The memorandum accounts are in separate subsidiary ledgers – sales ledger and purchases ledger.

■ At regular intervals control accounts are reconciled as follows:

– sales ledger control account to the total of the balances of the memorandum accounts in sales ledger

– purchases ledger control account to the total of the balances of the memorandum accounts in purchases ledger

– VAT control account to the amount due to or from HM Revenue & Customs

■ Control accounts are an aid to management:

– they give instant information on the total of receivables/payables/VAT

– by making fraud more difficult

– in helping to locate errors (but not all errors will be shown)

Key Terms		
control account	a 'master' account which controls a number of memorandum accounts
sales ledger control account	the 'master' account which controls the sales ledger
purchases ledger control account	the 'master' account which controls the purchases ledger
Value Added Tax control account	the account which brings together totals of VAT from the books of prime entry
set-off/contra entries	where balances in the sales ledger and the purchases ledger are set-off against one another
aged debtor analysis	a summary of each customer balance analysed into columns showing how long the amounts have been outstanding

Activities

8.1 You have the following information:

- opening customer balances at start of month £18,600
- credit sales for month £9,100
- sales returns for month £800

What is the figure for closing customer balances at the end of the month?

(a) £10,300

(b) £26,900

(c) £27,700

(d) £28,500

Answer (a) or (b) or (c) or (d)

8.2 Prepare a sales ledger control account for the month of June 20-7 from the following information:

20-7		£
1 Jun	Debit balance brought down	17,491
30 Jun	Credit sales for month	42,591
	Sales returns from credit customers	1,045
	Money received from credit customers	39,024

Balance the account at 30 June 20-7.

8.3 You work as an accounts assistant for Shire Traders. Today you are working on the sales ledger control account and sales ledger.

A summary of transactions with credit customers during June 20-5 is shown below.

	£
Goods sold on credit	118,600
Money received from credit customers	96,214
Discounts allowed	300
Goods returned by credit customers	650
Bad debt written off	350

The balance of customer accounts at 1 June 20-5 was £180,824.

(a) Prepare a sales ledger control account for the month of June 20-5 from the above details. Show clearly the balance carried down at 30 June 20-5.

Sales Ledger Control Account

Date 20-5	Details	Amount £	Date 20-5	Details	Amount £

The following memorandum account balances were in the sales ledger on 30 June 20-5:

	£	
Carless and Company	76,560	debit
BBT Limited	28,109	debit
Dale and Company	32,019	debit
Vale Computers	1,645	debit
Brandon Limited	350	debit
Bissell and Bradley	31,304	debit
Hopkins and Company	32,273	debit

(b) Reconcile these balances with the sales ledger control account balance you calculated in (a).

	£
Sales ledger control account balance as at 30 June 20-5	. . . .
Total of sales ledger accounts as at 30 June 20-5	. . . .
Difference	. . . .

(c)   What may have caused the difference calculated in (b)?

....

....

....

8.4   You work as an accounts assistant for Southtown Supplies. Today you are working on the sales ledger control account and sales ledger.

A summary of transactions with receivables (credit customers) in September 20-2 is shown below.

(a)   Show with a tick whether each entry will be a debit or credit in the sales ledger control account in the general ledger.

	Amount £	Debit ✔	Credit ✔
Balance of receivables at 1 September 20-2	47,238		
Goods sold on credit	31,054		
Money received from receivables	29,179		
Goods returned by receivables	2,684		
Discounts allowed	784		
Bad debt written off	450		

(b)   What will be the balance of receivables on 1 October 20-2 on the above account?

	✔
£44,295	
£45,195	
£45,645	
£46,095	

The balances in the sales ledger on 1 October 20-2 totalled £44,728

(c)   What is the difference between the total of the balances in the sales ledger and the sales ledger control account balance calculated in part (b)?

£
Workings:

(d)   Identify the two reasons, either of which might have caused the difference.

✔

Settlement discount has been understated in the sales ledger	
Goods returned have been understated in the sales ledger	
The bad debt written off has been omitted from the sales ledger	
Money received from customers has been overstated in the sales ledger	
Sales to credit customers have been overstated in the sales ledger	
Sales to credit customers have been understated in the sales ledger	
Trade discounts have not been included in the sales ledger	

8.5   You work as an accounts assistant for Bransford Supplies. Today you have printed out the aged debtor analysis as at 31 March 20-8, as follows:

Bransford Supplies Aged debtor analysis at 31 March 20-8				
Customer	Total	0-30 days	31-60 days	61+ days
	£	£	£	£
Benn Ltd	2,430	630	1,800	0
Charteris & Co	1,760	1,760	0	0
D Morgan	940	820	120	0
Wilson & Sons	3,610	0	0	3,610
Totals	8,740	3,210	1,920	3,610

For each of the customer accounts listed, indicate the action you suggest should be taken by the accounts supervisor.

	no action ✔	letter/email ✔	letter/email + phone call ✔
Benn Ltd			
Charteris & Co			
D Morgan			
Wilson & Sons			

8.6 You have the following information:

- opening supplier balances at start of month   £15,300
- credit purchases for month   £8,100
- purchases returns for month   £200

What is the figure for closing supplier balances at the end of the month?

(a) £7,000

(b) £7,400

(c) £23,200

(d) £23,600

Answer (a) or (b) or (c) or (d)

8.7 Prepare a purchases ledger control account for the month of April 20-9 from the following information:

20-9		£
1 Apr	Credit balance brought down	14,275
30 Apr	Credit purchases for month	36,592
	Purchases returns to credit suppliers	653
	Payments made to credit suppliers	31,074
	Contra entry (set-off against sales ledger control account)	597

Balance the account as at 30 April 20-9.

8.8 You work as an accounts assistant for Durning Traders. Today you are working on the purchases ledger control account and purchases ledger.

A summary of transactions with credit suppliers during May 20-3 is shown below.

	£
Goods purchased on credit	21,587
Payments made to credit suppliers	13,750
Discounts received	500
Goods returned to credit suppliers	250

The balance of suppliers at 1 May 20-3 was £50,300.

(a) Prepare a purchases ledger control account for the month of May 20-3 from the above details. Show clearly the balance carried down at 31 May 20-3.

Purchases Ledger Control Account

Date 20-3	Details	Amount £	Date 20-3	Details	Amount £

The following memorandum account balances were in the purchases ledger on 31 May 20-3:

Wright and Company	£12,000	credit
CCY Limited	£11,107	credit
Carter and Company	£9,380	credit
Tomkins Limited	£16,800	credit
PP Properties	£500	debit
L Vakas	£1,200	credit
Ten Traders	£6,400	credit

(b) Reconcile these balances with the purchases ledger control account balance you calculated in (a).

	£
Purchases ledger control account balance as at 31 May 20-3	. . . .
Total of purchases ledger accounts as at 31 May 20-3	. . . .
Difference	. . . .

(c)   What may have caused the difference calculated in (b)?

....

....

....

8.9   You work as an accounts assistant for Mawla Supplies. Today you are working on the purchases ledger control account and purchases ledger.

A summary of transactions with credit suppliers during August 20-4 is shown below.

(a)   Show whether each entry will be a debit or credit in the purchases ledger control account in the general ledger.

	Amount £	Debit ✔	Credit ✔
Balance of suppliers at 1 August 20-4	46,297		
Purchases from credit suppliers	22,084		
Payments made to credit suppliers	25,934		
Discounts received	425		
Goods returned to credit suppliers	1,108		

(b)   What will be the balance of credit suppliers on 1 September 20-4 on the above account?

	✔
£41,764	
£48,614	
£43,130	
£40,914	

The following credit balances were in the purchases ledger on 1 September 20-4.

	£
Perran Ltd	5,340
Chiverton & Co	2,195
Durning Builders	11,084
Chapelporth Ltd	7,319
Sennen & Co	3,107
Zelah plc	10,861

(c)   Reconcile the balances shown above with the purchases ledger control account balance calculated in part (b).

	£
Balance on purchases ledger control account at 1 September 20-4	
Total of the purchases ledger balances at 1 September 20-4	
Difference	

(d)   Which one of the following errors may have caused the difference calculated in part (c)?

	✔
An invoice was entered twice in the purchases ledger	
A credit note was not entered in the purchases ledger	
A credit note was entered twice in the purchases ledger control account	
A credit note was not entered in the purchases ledger control account	

8.10   Indicate whether the following will be recorded as debits or credits in VAT control account:

	debit ✔	credit ✔
VAT on credit purchases		
VAT on cash sales		
VAT on purchases returns		
VAT on credit sales		
VAT on sales returns		

8.11   You work as an accounts assistant for Blenheim Builders. Today you are working on VAT control account.

The following figures have been taken from Blenheim Builders' books of prime entry for the three months ended 30 June 20-4:

Sales day book	
Net	£56,000
VAT	£9,800
Gross	£65,800

Purchases day book	
Net	£23,200
VAT	£4,060
Gross	£27,260

Sales returns day book	
Net	£1,440
VAT	£252
Gross	£1,692

Purchases returns day book	
Net	£1,120
VAT	£196
Gross	£1,316

Cash book: cash sales	
Net	£2,480
VAT	£434
Gross	£2,914

(a)   From the books of prime entry, write up the VAT control account of Blenheim Builders for the three months ended 30 June 20-4.

VAT Control Account

Date 20-4	Details	Amount £	Date 20-4	Details	Amount £

(b)   Balance VAT control account at 30 June 20-4 and show the balance brought down on 1 July 20-4.

(c)   The VAT Return calculation has been completed by another accounts assistant and shows an amount owing to HM Revenue & Customs of £6,370.

Is the VAT return correct?   Yes/No

If it is not correct, what do you think has caused the error?

9 The journal

this chapter covers...

The journal is the book of prime entry for non-regular accounting transactions. Like other books of prime entry – eg sales day book – the journal is used to list transactions before they are entered into the double-entry book-keeping system.

In this chapter we will see how the journal is used for non-regular transactions such as:

- opening entries (the first transactions to open the accounts of a new business)
- bad debt write off (where a customer's account is to be written off as irrecoverable)
- payroll transactions (the accounting entries which record wages and salaries paid to employees)

A further use of the journal is to show the entries required to correct errors found in the accounting system – this topic of correction of errors is covered in the next chapter.

USE OF THE JOURNAL

The journal completes the accounting system by providing the book of prime entry for non-regular transactions which are not recorded in any other book of prime entry. Such non-regular transactions include:

- opening entries
- bad debt write off
- payroll transactions
- correction of errors (see Chapter 10)

The reasons for using a journal are:

- to provide a book of prime entry for non-regular transactions
- to eliminate the need for remembering why non-regular transactions were put through the accounts – the journal acts as a notebook
- to reduce the risk of fraud, by making it difficult for unauthorised transactions to be entered in the accounting system
- to reduce the risk of errors, by listing the transactions that are to be put into the double-entry accounts
- to ensure that entries can be traced back to an authorised financial document (note that documentation is stored securely for possible future reference)

THE JOURNAL – A BOOK OF PRIME ENTRY

The journal is a book of prime entry; it is not, therefore, part of the double-entry book-keeping system. The journal is used to list the transactions that are to be put through the accounts. The accounting system for non-regular transactions is as follows:

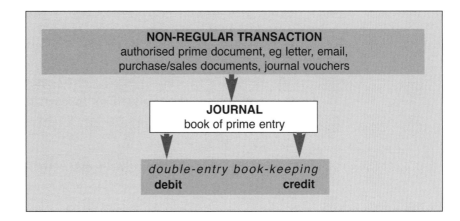

The journal is set out in the following way, with a sample transaction:

Date	Details	Reference	Dr	Cr
20-4			£	£
1 Jul	Bank	CB	20,000	
	Capital	GL		20,000
	Opening capital introduced			

Notes:

- journal entries are prepared from authorised financial documents (which are stored securely for possible future reference)
- the names of the accounts to be debited and credited in the accounting system are written in the details column; it is customary to show the debit transaction first
- the money amount of each debit and credit entry is stated in the appropriate column
- the reference column shows where each account is found, and often includes an account number (eg CB = Cash Book, GL = General Ledger)
- a journal entry always balances, ie debit and credit entries are for the same amount or total
- it is usual to include a brief narrative (ie a few words) explaining why the transaction is being carried out, and making reference to the financial document whenever possible (you should always include a narrative unless specifically told otherwise)
- each journal entry is complete in itself and is ruled off to separate it from the next entry

Note that any transactions involving sales ledger control account and purchases ledger control account must also be recorded in the memorandum accounts in sales ledger and purchases ledger respectively.

OPENING ENTRIES

Opening entries are the transactions to open the accounts of a new business.

An example of an opening entry is:

1 Jan 20-4 Started in business with £10,000 in the bank

This non-regular transaction is entered in the journal as follows:

Date	Details	Reference	Dr	Cr
20-4			£	£
1 Jan	Bank	CB	10,000	
	Capital	GL		10,000
	Opening capital introduced			

After the journal entry has been made, the transaction is recorded in the double-entry accounts, as follows:

GENERAL LEDGER

Dr				**Cash Book**				Cr
20-4	Details	Cash	Bank	20-4	Details	Cash	Bank
		£	£			£	£
1 Jan	Capital		10,000				

Dr		**Capital Account**		Cr
20-4		£	20-4	£
			1 Jan Bank	10,000

Here is another opening entries transaction to be recorded in the journal:

1 Feb 20-4   *Started in business with cash £100, bank £5,000, inventory (stock) £1,000, machinery £2,500, creditors £850*

The journal entry is:

Date	Details	Reference	Dr	Cr
20-4			£	£
1 Feb	Cash	CB	100	
	Bank	CB	5,000	
	Inventory (stock)	GL	1,000	
	Machinery	GL	2,500	
	Purchases ledger control	GL		850
	Capital*	GL		7,750
			8,600	8,600
	Assets and liabilities			
	at the start of business			

* Assets – liabilities = capital (ie 100 + 5,000 + 1,000 + 2,500 – 850 = 7,750)

Notes:

- capital is, in this example, the balancing figure, ie assets minus liabilities
- the journal is the book of prime entry for all opening entries, including cash and bank; however the normal book of prime entry for other cash/bank transactions is the cash book
- the amounts for the journal entry will now need to be recorded in the double-entry accounts as follows:

GENERAL LEDGER

Dr				Cash Book			Cr	
20-4	Details	Cash	Bank	20-4	Details	Cash	Bank
1 Feb	Capital	£ 100	£ 5,000			£	£

Dr	Inventory (Stock) Account		Cr
20-4		£	20-4	£
1 Feb	Capital	1,000	

Dr	Machinery Account		Cr
20-4		£	20-4	£
1 Feb	Capital	2,500	

Dr	Purchases Ledger Control Account		Cr
20-4		£	20-4	£
			1 Feb	Capital	850

Dr	Capital Account		Cr
20-4		£	20-4	£
			1 Feb	Journal	7,750

- the individual amounts making up the £850 recorded in purchases ledger control account must be recorded in the memorandum accounts in purchases ledger

- the cross-reference in capital account is to the journal – in this way it is possible to refer back to the journal entry to see the assets and liabilities which formed the opening capital of the business; alternatively, individual amounts of the opening assets and liabilities could be recorded in capital account and cross-referenced with the name of their general ledger account

BAD DEBT WRITE OFF

A bad debt is a debt owing to a business which it considers will never be paid.

One of the problems of selling goods and services on credit terms is that, from time-to-time, some customers will not pay. As a consequence, the balances of such customers' accounts have to be written off when they become irrecoverable (uncollectable). This happens when all efforts to recover the amounts owing have been exhausted, ie statements and letters have been sent to the customer requesting payment, and legal action – where appropriate – or the threat of legal action, has failed to obtain payment.

In writing off a customer's account as bad, the business is bearing the cost of the amount due. The customer's account is written off as bad and the amount is debited to bad debts written off account.

Towards the financial year-end it is good practice for the accounts supervisor (or other authorised person) to go through the customers' accounts to see if any need to be written off. The accounts supervisor will then advise the accounts assistant which accounts are to be written off (the advice – often in the form of an email – forms the prime document for the bad debt write-off).

We have already seen, in Chapter 8, the double-entry book-keeping entries to write off a customer's account:
- *debit* bad debts account
- *debit* Value Added Tax account
- *credit* sales ledger control account (and credit the memorandum account of the customer in sales ledger)

For example:

15 Dec 20-4   *The accounts supervisor emails you telling you to write off the account of Don's Diner, which has a balance of £47 (including VAT), as a bad debt*

The journal entry is:

Date	Details	Reference	Dr	Cr
20-4			£	£
15 Dec	Bad debts	GL	40	
	Value Added Tax	GL	7	
	Sales ledger control	GL		47
			47	47
	Balance of memorandum sales ledger account of Don's Diner written off as a bad debt, as per email from accounts supervisor			

After the journal entry has been made, the transaction is recorded in the double-entry accounts as follows:

GENERAL LEDGER

Dr			**Bad Debts Account**		Cr
20-4		£	20-4		£
15 Dec	Sales ledger control	40			

Dr			**Value Added Tax Account**		Cr
20-4		£	20-4		£
15 Dec	Sales ledger control	7			

Dr			**Sales Ledger Control Account**		Cr
20-4		£	20-4		£
			15 Dec	Bad debts/VAT	47

In sales ledger, the memorandum account of Don's Diner is recorded as follows:

SALES LEDGER

Dr			**Don's Diner**		Cr
20-4		£	20-4		£
1 Dec	Balance b/d	47	15 Dec	Bad debts/VAT	47

With the debt written off, this account now has a nil balance.

PAYROLL TRANSACTIONS

what is meant by payroll transactions?

Payroll transactions are the accounting entries which record wages and salaries paid to employees.

Payroll transactions require journal and accounting entries for:

–   gross pay
–   net pay
–   income tax
–   employer's National Insurance contributions
–   employees' National Insurance contributions
–   employer's pension contributions
–   employees' pension contributions
–   voluntary deductions from employees' pay

what payroll transactions are entered in the accounts?

The payroll transactions to be entered into the accounts are:

*   **gross pay**, which is the amount of employees' pay before any deductions

*   **net pay**, which is the amount paid to employees after deductions for income tax, employees' National Insurance contributions, employees' pension fund contributions and voluntary deductions

*   **income tax** collected by the employer and paid to HM Revenue & Customs

*   **employer's National Insurance** contributions paid to HM Revenue & Customs

*   **employees' National Insurance** contributions collected by the employer and paid to the HM Revenue & Customs

*   **pension contributions provided by the employer** and paid to pension funds

*   **employees' pension contributions** deducted from employees' pay and paid to pension funds

*   **voluntary deductions**, eg trade union fees, deducted from employees' pay and paid to the organisation

accounts used in payroll transactions

The double-entry accounts used to record payroll transactions are:

bank

This records:

- payment of the net pay of employees

- payment to outside agencies – the deductions to HM Revenue & Customs, payments to pension funds, and payments for voluntary deductions

wages control account

This is the main account for payroll – all transactions for payroll pass through this account which forms one-half of the double-entry – a debit or credit to wages control account will be a credit or debit in one of the other payroll accounts

wages expense

This is the employer's expense account for paying employees which records:

- employees' gross pay

- employer's National Insurance Contributions

- employer's pension and voluntary contributions (if there are any)

HM Revenue & Customs

This records amounts payable to the HM Revenue & Customs for income tax and National Insurance contributions

pension fund

This records amounts payable to external pension funds: the employer's and employees' contributions

wages control account

The diagram below shows the relationship of wages control account and the other payroll accounts. Note that the bank account is not shown here – it is involved in many of the transactions, as we will see in the Case Study on the next page.

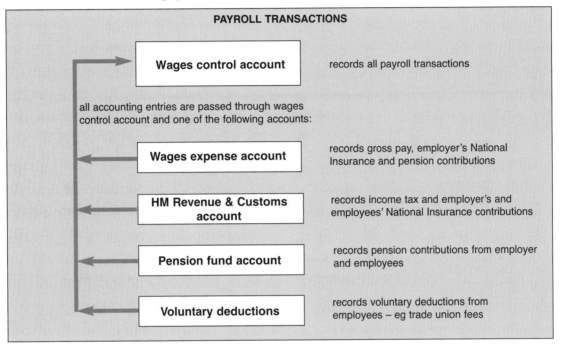

PAYROLL TRANSACTIONS

Wages control account	records all payroll transactions

all accounting entries are passed through wages control account and one of the following accounts:

Wages expense account	records gross pay, employer's National Insurance and pension contributions
HM Revenue & Customs account	records income tax and employer's and employees' National Insurance contributions
Pension fund account	records pension contributions from employer and employees
Voluntary deductions	records voluntary deductions from employees – eg trade union fees

journal and ledger entries

Payroll transactions must be recorded by means of a journal entry in order to be able to trace the accounting entries from the payroll records (the financial document), through the book of prime entry (the journal) to the general ledger accounts.

As payroll is quite complex it is best to take a step-by-step approach (which is used in the Case Study on the next page). The journal entries and ledger entries are as follows:

1. Record the wages expense (the total cost to the employer)
2. Record the net pay (to be paid to employees)
3. Record the liability to HM Revenue & Customs (for income tax and National Insurance contributions)
4. Record the liability to the pension fund (both employer and employee contributions)
5. Record the liability for voluntary deductions, eg trade union fees

The Case Study which follows illustrates this step-by-step approach.

Case Study

1.850

1.600

PAYROLL TRANSACTIONS

situation

Matrix is a small business employing five staff. It operates a monthly payroll which is run on the last day of the month. Payroll figures for November 20-8 are:

gross pay	£5,500
net pay	£3,820
income tax	£900
employer's National Insurance contributions	£550
employees' National Insurance contributions	£450
employer's pension contributions	£275
employees' pension contributions	£275
voluntary deductions: trade union fees	£55

We will now see the journal and general ledger entries for these payroll transactions, taking a step-by-step approach.

solution

These are the payments that are due for the November payroll of Matrix.

payments due to the employees

Gross pay	£5,500	
less		
Income tax	£900	
National Insurance	£450	
Pension contributions	£275	
Trade union fees	£55	
Net pay due		£3,820

payment due to HM Revenue & Customs

Income tax deducted from pay	£900	
Employer's National Insurance contributions	£550	
Employees' National Insurance contributions	£450	
		£1,900

payment due to the pension fund

Employer's contributions	£275	
Employees' contributions, deducted from pay	£275	
		£550

payment due to voluntary deductions

Employees' payment, for trade union fees, deducted from pay		£55
payments total		**£6,325**

The four amounts, shown in the right-hand column on the previous page, are recorded in the journal and entered into the general ledger accounts. This is done as follows:

Step 1

Transfer the total of the payments (here £6,325) to wages account (this is the cost to the employer) and to wages control account.

Journal

Date	Details	Reference	Dr	Cr
20-8			£	£
30 Nov	Wages expense		6,325	
	Wages control			6,325
	Transfer of wages expense			

Dr	**Wages Expense Account**			Cr
20-8		£	20-8	£
30 Nov	Wages control	6,325		

Dr	**Wages Control Account**			Cr
20-8		£	20-8	£
			30 Nov Wages expense	6,325

Note: this total agrees with the payments total of £6,325 (shown on the previous page) which is the total payroll expense to the business for the month.

Step 2

Make entries for the payment of wages (the net pay paid from the bank).

Journal

Date	Details	Reference	Dr	Cr
20-8			£	£
30 Nov	Wages control		3,820	
	Bank			3,820
	Net wages paid to employees			

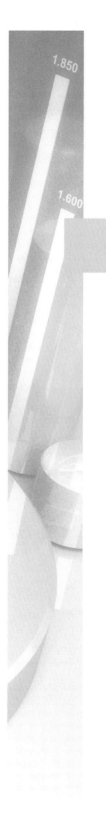

Dr		**Wages Control Account**		Cr
20-8		£	20-8	£
30 Nov	Bank	3,820	30 Nov Wages expense	6,325

Dr		**Bank Account**		Cr
20-8		£	20-8	£
			30 Nov Wages control	3,820

Step 3

Transfer the amount due to HMRC to HM Revenue & Customs account.

Journal

Date	Details	Reference	Dr	Cr
20-8			£	£
30 Nov	Wages control		1,900	
	HM Revenue & Customs			1,900
	Amount due to HMRC			

The amount due is £1,900 and comprises income tax £900 and National Insurance contributions – employer's £550 and employees' £450.

Dr		**Wages Control Account**		Cr
20-8		£	20-8	£
30 Nov	Bank	3,820	30 Nov Wages expense	6,325
30 Nov	HM Revenue & Customs	1,900		

Dr		**HM Revenue & Customs Account**		Cr
20-8		£	20-8	£
			30 Nov Wages control	1,900

Note: This account shows HM Revenue & Customs as a payable (creditor) of the business. The liability will be paid by the business (*debit* HM Revenue & Customs, *credit* bank) during the next month.

Step 4
Transfer the amount due to the pension fund.

The amount due is £550 – employer's contribution £275, employee's contribution £275.

Journal

Date	Details	Reference	Dr	Cr
20-8			£	£
30 Nov	Wages control		550	
	Pension fund			550
	Amount due to pension fund			

Dr		**Wages Control Account**			Cr
20-8			£	20-8	£
30 Nov	Bank		3,820	30 Nov Wages expense	6,325
30 Nov	HM Revenue & Customs		1,900		
30 Nov	Pension fund		550		

Dr		**Pension Fund Account**		Cr
20-8		£	20-8	£
			30 Nov Wages control	550

Note: This account shows the pension fund as a creditor of the business. The liability will be paid by the business (*debit* pension fund, *credit* bank) when payment is made to the pension fund provider during the next month.

Step 5
Transfer the amount due for voluntary deductions.

The amount due is £55, being the trade union fees.

Journal

Date	Details	Reference	Dr	Cr
20-8			£	£
30 Nov	Wages control		55	
	Trade union fees			55
	Amount due for trade union fees			

Dr			Wages Control Account		Cr
20-8		£	20-8		£
30 Nov	Bank	3,820	30 Nov Wages expense		6,325
30 Nov	HM Revenue & Customs	1,900			
30 Nov	Pension fund	550			
30 Nov	Trade union fees	55			
		6,325			6,325

Dr		Trade Union Fees Account		Cr
20-8		£	20-8	£
			30 Nov Wages control	55

Note: This account shows that trade union fees as a creditor of the business. The liability will be paid by the business (*debit* trade union fees, *credit* bank) when payment is made to the trade union during the next month.

conclusion

You will see from the journal and accounting entries shown above that the wages control account records all the payroll accounting transactions carried out each time the payroll is run. At the end of the process the control account balance reverts to zero – you will see above that the total of both sides after Step 5 transfer is £6,325 – ie the balance is nil.

MAKING JOURNAL ENTRIES

As we have seen in this chapter, the journal is the book of prime entry for non-regular transactions. Because of the irregular nature of journal transactions, it is important that they are correctly authorised by the appropriate person – such as the accounts supervisor, the administration manager, the owner of the business. The authorisation will, ideally, be a financial document – eg letter, email or other document – but may well be verbal – eg "write-off the account of Zelah Limited as a bad debt."

It is good practice to ensure that journal entries are checked by an appropriate person before they are entered into the double-entry book-keeping system. It is all too easy to get a journal entry the wrong way round resulting in an error.

In the next chapter we will look at the use of the journal when correcting errors in the accounting system.

■ The journal is used to list non-regular transactions.

■ The journal is a book of prime entry – it is not a double-entry account.

■ Journal entries are prepared from authorised financial documents, which are stored securely for possible future reference.

■ The journal is used for:
  – opening entries
  – bad debt write off
  – payroll transactions
  – correction of errors (see Chapter 10)

■ Payroll transactions require journal and accounting entries for:
  – gross pay
  – net pay
  – income tax
  – employer's and employees' National Insurance contributions
  – employer's and employees' pension contributions
  – voluntary deductions from employees' pay

journal	the book of prime entry for non-regular transactions
opening entries	the transactions to open the accounts of a new business
bad debt	a debt owing to a business which it considers will never be paid
payroll transactions	the accounting entries which record wages and salaries paid to employees
wages control account	the main account for payroll through which all transactions for payroll pass
gross pay	the amount of employees' pay before any deductions
net pay	the amount paid to employees after deductions for income tax, employees' National Insurance contributions, employees' pension fund contributions, and voluntary deductions
HM Revenue & Customs	receives amounts from payroll in respect of income tax, employer's National Insurance contributions, and employees' National Insurance contribution

Activities

9.1 Hussain Limited is a furniture manufacturer. Which one of the following transactions will be recorded in the journal?

(a)   sale of furniture on credit to a customer

(b)   cash purchase of fabric for chair seat covers

(c)   write off of credit customer's account from sales ledger as a bad debt

(d)   petty cash purchase of postage stamps

Answer (a) or (b) or (c) or (d)

9.2 Which one of the following will not be recorded in the journal?

(a)   payroll transactions

(b)   cash sale of goods

(c)   write off of a bad debt

(d)   opening entries

Answer (a) or (b) or (c) or (d)

9.3 Which financial transaction goes with which book of prime entry?

financial transaction
- opening entries for a new business
- credit purchase of goods from a supplier
- returned credit purchases to the supplier
- customer returns goods sold on credit
- BACS receipt from a customer
- credit sale of goods to a customer
- expense paid out of petty cash

book of prime entry
- petty cash book
- sales day book
- purchases day book
- sales returns day book
- purchases returns day book
- journal
- cash book

9.4 Lucy Wallis started in business on 1 May 20-8 with the following assets and liabilities:

	£
Vehicle	6,500
Fixtures and fittings	2,800
Inventory (stock)	4,100
Bank	150
Loan from husband	5,000

You are to prepare Lucy's opening journal entry, showing clearly her capital at 1 May 20-8.

9.5 Jane Seymour is setting up a new business and has listed all the accounts and their amounts that will be used. She asks you to complete the journal entry by ticking the appropriate column in the table below, and to calculate her opening capital.

Account name	Amount	Debit	Credit
	£	✔	✔
Cash	200		
Cash at bank	2,340		
Capital			
Payables	3,985		
Receivables	4,751		
Loan from bank	12,650		
Office equipment	4,120		
Rent paid	950		
Inventory (stock)	2,310		
Sundry expenses	1,194		
Vehicles	8,350		
Wages	2,294		

9.6 You are an accounts assistant at Baxter Limited. The accounts supervisor has sent you an email instructing you to write off as a bad debt the account of Boughton and Company, a credit customer who owes £240 plus VAT. Which one of the following sets of transactions will you make in the general ledger?

(a)   debit bad debts £282; credit VAT £42; credit sales ledger control £240

(b)   debit sales ledger control £282; credit bad debts £282

(c)   debit bad debts £240; debit VAT £42; credit bank £282

(d)   debit bad debts £240; debit VAT £42; credit sales ledger control £282

Answer (a) or (b) or (c) or (d)

9.7   You are employed by Tyax Trading as an accounts assistant. Today the accounts supervisor sends you the following email:

EMAIL

To   accountsassistant@tyax.co.uk

From   accountssupervisor@tyax.co.uk

Subject   Sales Ledger: Smithers and Sons

The above credit customer has ceased trading, owing us £840 plus VAT. Please record the journal entries needed in general ledger to write off as a bad debt the net amount and the VAT. Use the layout below.

Account name	Amount	Debit	Credit
	£	✔	✔

The following information is used in multiple-choice questions 9.8 to 9.10. In each case, choose one option from (a) to (d)

The payroll system of Home Fires Limited has recorded the following totals for the month of July:

gross pay	£350,780
income tax	£69,500
employer's National Insurance contributions	£35,085
employees' National Insurance contributions	£31,450
employer's pension contributions	£7,500
employees' pension contributions	£7,500
trade union fees	£1,500

9.8   The total payment to the HM Revenue & Customs for the month is:

(a)   £100,950

(b)   £104,585

(c)   £15,000

(d)   £136,035

9.9 The total wages expense to the employer is:

(a) £350,780

(b) £462,865

(c) £393,365

(d) £308,195

9.10 The total net pay to employees is:

(a) £240,830

(b) £248,330

(c) £388,230

(d) £349,280

9.11 Pegasus Limited has recorded the following payroll totals for the month of October 20-3:

gross pay	£101,500
income tax	£20,500
employer's National Insurance contributions	£10,150
employees' National Insurance contributions	£9,860
trade union fees	£850

You are to:

(a) Calculate the total payroll cost to the employer

(b) Calculate the payment due to HM Revenue & Customs

(c) Calculate the net pay due to employees

(d) Prepare journals dated 31 October 20-3 to show the entries needed in general ledger to record:

· the wages expense

· the liability to MH Revenue & Customs

· the net wages paid to employees

· the liability for trade union fees

9.12 Jason's Wool Shop has recorded the following payroll totals for the month of January 20-5:

gross pay	£50,000
income tax	£11,110
employer's National Insurance contributions	£5,010
employees' National Insurance contributions	£4,985
employer's pension contributions	£1,100
employees' pension contributions	£1,100

Jason's Wool Shop uses the following general ledger accounts for payroll transactions: wages control, wages expense, bank, HM Revenue & Customs, and pension fund.

You are to:

Use the journals below to show the entries needed in general ledger to:

(a) record the wages expense

(b) record the liability to HM Revenue & Customs

(c) record the net wages paid to the employees

(d) record the liability to the pension fund

(a)

Account name	Amount £	Debit ✔	Credit ✔

(b)

Account name	Amount £	Debit ✔	Credit ✔

(c)

Account name	Amount £	Debit ✔	Credit ✔

(d)

Account name	Amount £	Debit ✔	Credit ✔

10 The trial balance and correction of errors

The trial balance lists the balances of every account from the ledger, distinguishing between those accounts which have debit balances and those which have credit balances.

The debit balances and credit balances are totalled and, when the two totals are the same, this proves that the accounting records are arithmetically correct. The initial trial balance has been covered in the learning area for Basic Accounting I.

A trial balance does not prove the complete accuracy of the accounting records and there may well be errors. These fall into two groups:

- *errors not shown by a trial balance*
- *errors shown by a trial balance*

In this chapter, we look at the types of errors within each of these groups and, when they are found, we explain how to correct them using journal entries and see how the trial balance is affected.

EXTRACTING A TRIAL BALANCE

An initial trial balance is extracted from the accounting records in order to make an initial check of the arithmetical accuracy of the double-entry book-keeping, ie that the debit entries equal the credit entries.

A trial balance is a list of the balances of every account from general ledger (including cash book and petty cash book), distinguishing between those accounts which have debit balances and those which have credit balances.

A trial balance is extracted at regular intervals – often at the end of each month – and the balances are set out in two totalled columns, a debit column and a credit column. The debit and credit columns are totalled and the totals should agree. In this way the trial balance proves that the accounting records are arithmetically correct. However, a trial balance does not prove the complete accuracy of the accounting records as there may well be errors – which we will look at in this chapter.

An example of a trial balance is shown below.

Trial balance of Ace Suppliers as at 31 January 20-4	Dr £	Cr £
Name of account		
Purchases	7,500	
Sales		16,000
Sales returns	250	
Purchases returns		500
Sales ledger control	1,550	
Purchases ledger control		900
Rent	1,000	
Wages	1,500	
Heating and lighting	1,250	
Office equipment	5,000	
Machinery	7,500	
Inventory (Stock) at 1 Jan 20-4	2,500	
Petty cash	200	
Bank	4,850	
Value Added Tax		1,200
J Williams: loan		7,000
Capital		10,000
Drawings	2,500	
	35,600	35,600

ERRORS IN THE ACCOUNTING SYSTEM

In any accounting system there is always the possibility of errors. As noted in the previous section, a trial balance does not prove the complete accuracy of the accounting records and there may well be errors.

Ways to avoid errors, or ways to reveal them sooner, include:

- division of the accounting function between a number of people, so that no one person is responsible for all aspects of a business transaction
- regular circulation of statements of account to customers, who will check the transactions on their accounts and advise any discrepancies
- checking of statements of account received from suppliers against the accounting records
- extraction of a trial balance at regular intervals
- the checking of bank statements and preparing bank reconciliation statements
- checking cash and petty cash balances against cash held
- the use of control accounts
- the use of a computer accounting program

Despite all of these precautions, errors will still occur from time-to-time.

We will look at:

- correction of errors not shown by a trial balance
- correction of errors shown by a trial balance, using a suspense account

We will look at each of these two groups and will see the journal entry needed to correct the various types of errors, together with the ledger entries and the effect on the trial balance.

ERRORS NOT SHOWN BY A TRIAL BALANCE

As mentioned earlier, a trial balance does not prove the complete accuracy of the accounting records.

There are six types of errors that are not shown by a trial balance, as follows:

error of omission

Here a financial transaction has been completely omitted from the accounting records, ie both the debit and credit entries have not been made.

error of commission

Here, a transaction is entered to the wrong person's account. For example, a sale of goods on credit to T Hughes has been entered as debit to J Hughes' account. Double-entry book-keeping has been completed and the sales ledger control account will reconcile with the sales ledger. However, when J Hughes receives a statement of account, he or she will soon complain about being debited with goods not ordered or received.

error of principle

This is when a transaction has been entered in the wrong type of account. For example, the cost of fuel for vehicles has been entered as debit vehicles account, credit bank account. The error is that vehicles account is a non-current (fixed asset), and the transaction should have been debited to the expense account for vehicle running expenses. If not corrected such an error of principle will show a false financial position for the business.

error of original entry

Here, the correct accounts have been used, and the correct sides: what is wrong is that the amount has been entered incorrectly in both accounts. This could be caused by a 'bad figure' on an invoice or a cheque, or it could be caused by a 'reversal of figures', eg an amount of £45 being entered in both accounts as £54. Note that both debit and credit entries need to be made incorrectly for the trial balance still to balance; if one entry has been made incorrectly and the other is correct, then the error will be shown.

reversal of entries

With this error, the debit and credit entries have been made in the accounts but on the wrong side of the two accounts concerned. For example, a cash sale has been entered wrongly as debit sales account, credit cash account. (This should have been entered as a debit to cash account, and a credit to sales account.)

compensating error

This is where two errors cancel each other out. For example, if the balance of purchases account is calculated wrongly at £10 too much, and a similar error has occurred in calculating the balance of sales account, then the two errors will compensate each other, and the trial balance will not show the errors.

Although these errors are not shown by a trial balance, they are likely to come to light if the procedures suggested on the previous page, are followed. For example, a customer will soon let you know if their account has been debited with goods they did not buy.

When an error is found, it needs to be corrected by means of a journal entry which shows the correcting book-keeping entries. Remember that all journal entries are prepared from authorised financial documents – these could take the form of an email or a note from the accounts supervisor; such documents, together with any other paperwork, should be stored securely for possible future reference.

We will now look at an example of each of the errors not shown by a trial balance, and will see how it is corrected by means of a journal entry.

A practical hint which may help in correcting errors is to write out the double-entry accounts as they appear with the error; then write in the correcting entries and see if the result has achieved what was intended.

ERRORS NOT SHOWN BY THE TRIAL BALANCE: JOURNAL ENTRIES

We will now discuss the errors which are not shown by a trial balance and see an example journal entry for each. Remember that:

- the journal is the book of prime entry for non-regular transactions
- journal entries must be recorded in the accounting system
- for journal entries which involve sales ledger control account or purchases ledger control account, the transactions must also be recorded in the memorandum accounts in the subsidiary ledger – either sales ledger or purchases ledger

For each example error, the correcting journal and ledger entries are shown.

error of omission

Credit sale of goods, £200 plus VAT (at 17.5%) on invoice 4967 to H Jarvis completely omitted from the accounting system; the error is corrected on 12 May 20-4.

Date	Details	Reference	Dr	Cr
20-4			£	£
12 May	Sales ledger control	GL	235	
	Sales	GL		200
	VAT	GL		35
			235	235
	Invoice 4967 omitted from accounts: in the sales ledger – debit H Jarvis £235			

GENERAL LEDGER

Dr **Sales Ledger Control Account** Cr

20-4		£	20-4		£
12 May	Sales/VAT	235			

Dr **Sales Account** Cr

20-4		£	20-4		£
			12 May	Sales ledger control	200

Dr **Value Added Tax Account** Cr

20-4		£	20-4		£
			12 May	Sales ledger control	35

SALES LEDGER

Dr **H Jarvis** Cr

20-4		£	20-4		£
12 May	Sales/VAT	235			

Note: the cross reference in the accounts here is to 'journal' because the correcting journal entry refers to several accounts.

An error of omission can happen in a very small business – often where the book-keeping is done by one person: for example, an invoice is 'lost' down the back of a filing cabinet. Where a computer accounting system is used, it should be impossible for this error to occur. Also, if documents are numbered in sequence, then none should be mislaid.

error of commission

Credit sales of £47, including VAT (at 17.5%) on invoice no 321 have been debited to the account of J Adams, instead of the account of J Adams Limited; the error is corrected on 17 May 20-4.

Date	Details	Reference	Dr	Cr
20-4			£	£
17 May	Sales ledger control	GL	47	
	Sales ledger control	GL		47
	Correction of error (invoice 321):			
	in the sales ledger			
	– debit J Adams Limited £47			
	– credit J Adams £47			

GENERAL LEDGER

Dr	Sales Ledger Control Account			Cr
20-4		£	20-4	£
17 May	Sales ledger control	47	17 May Sales ledger control	47

SALES LEDGER

Dr	J Adams Limited			Cr
20-4		£	20-4	£
17 May	J Adams	47		

Dr	J Adams			Cr
20-4		£	20-4	£
			17 May J Adams Limited	47

An error of commission can be avoided, to some extent, by the use of account numbers, and by persuading the customer to quote the account number or reference on each transaction. All computer accounting systems use numbers/references to identify accounts, but it is still possible to post a transaction to the wrong account.

error of principle

The cost of diesel fuel, £50 (excluding VAT) on receipt no 34535, has been debited to vehicles account; the error is corrected on 20 May 2004.

Date	Details	Reference	Dr	Cr
20-4			£	£
20 May	Vehicle expenses	GL	50	
	Vehicles	GL		50
	Correction of error: receipt 34535			

GENERAL LEDGER

Dr	Vehicle Expenses Account			Cr
20-4		£	20-4	£
20 May	Vehicles	50		

Dr	**Vehicles Account**		Cr
20-4	£	20-4	£
		20 May Vehicle expenses	50

An error of principle is similar to an error of commission except that, instead of the wrong person's account being used, it is the wrong class of account.

In the above example, the vehicle running costs must be kept separate from the cost of the asset (the vehicle), otherwise the expense and asset accounts will be incorrect, leading to the ledger accounts showing a false financial position for the business.

error of original entry

Postages of £45 paid by cheque entered in the accounts as £54; the error is corrected on 27 May 20-4.

Do not correct an error like this by putting an amount for the difference through the accounts – here by debiting bank and crediting postages with £9. The reason for saying this is that there was no original transaction for this amount. Instead we must make two journal entries to:

- remove the incorrect entry
- record the correct entry

In this example, the journal entries are:

Date	Details	Reference	Dr	Cr
20-4			£	£
27 May	Bank	CB	54	
	Postages	GL		54
	Removing the incorrect entry:			
	transaction entered as £54			
	instead of £45			

Date	Details	Reference	Dr	Cr
20-4			£	£
27 May	Postages	GL	45	
	Bank	CB		45
	Recording the correct entry:			
	transaction entered as £54			
	instead of £45			

GENERAL LEDGER

Dr **Cash Book** (bank columns) Cr

20-4		£	20-4		£
27 May	Postages	54	27 May	Postages	45

Dr **Postages Account** Cr

20-4		£	20-4		£
27 May	Bank	45	27 May	Bank	54

A reversal of figures either has a difference of nine (as above), or an amount divisible by nine. An error of original entry can also be a 'bad' figure on a cheque or an invoice, entered wrongly into both accounts.

reversal of entries

A payment, on 3 May 20-4 by cheque for £50 to a supplier, S Wright (cheque no 093459), has been debited in the cash book and credited to purchases ledger control account; this is corrected on 12 May 20-4.

This error is corrected by two journal entries. Although the error here could be corrected by debiting purchases ledger control account and crediting bank with £100, there was no original transaction for this amount. Instead we must make two journal entries to:

- remove the incorrect entry
- record the correct entry

In this example the journal entries are:

Date	Details	Reference	Dr	Cr
20-4			£	£
12 May	Purchases ledger control	GL	50	
	Bank	CB		50
	Removing the incorrect entry			
	(cheque no 093459):			
	in the purchases ledger debit			
	S Wright £50			

Date	Details	Reference	Dr	Cr
20-4			£	£
12 May	Purchases ledger control	GL	50	
	Bank	CB		50
	Recording the correct entry			
	(cheque no 093459):			
	in the purchases ledger debit			
	S Wright £50			

It is often an idea to write out the accounts, complete with the error, and then to write in the correcting entries. The two accounts involved in this last error are shown with the error made on 3 May, and the corrections made on 12 May indicated by the shading:

GENERAL LEDGER

Dr			**Purchases Ledger Control Account**		Cr
20-4		£	20-4		£
12 May	Bank	50	3 May	Bank	50
12 May	Bank	50			

Dr			**Cash Book** (bank columns)		Cr
20-4		£	20-4		£
3 May	S Wright	50	12 May	S Wright	50
			12 May	S Wright	50

The accounts now show a net debit transaction of £50 on purchases ledger control account, and a net credit transaction of £50 on bank account, which is how this payment to a supplier should have been recorded in the first place.

compensating error

Rent account is overcast (ie it is over-added) by £100; sales account is also overcast by the same amount; the error is corrected on 31 May 20-4.

Date	Details	Reference	Dr	Cr
20-4			£	£
31 May	Sales	GL	100	
	Rent	GL		100
	Correction of overcast on rent			
	account and sales account			

GENERAL LEDGER

Dr	Sales Account		Cr
20-4	£	20-4	£
31 May Rent	100		

Dr	Rent Account		Cr
20-4	£	20-4	£
		31 May Sales	100

In this example, an account with a debit balance – rent – has been overcast; this is compensated by an overcast on an account with a credit balance – sales. There are several permutations on this theme, eg two debit balances, one overcast, one undercast; a debit balance undercast, a credit balance undercast.

TRIAL BALANCE ERRORS: USE OF SUSPENSE ACCOUNT

There are six types of errors which are revealed by a trial balance:

- calculation errors in ledger accounts
- single entry transactions
- recording two debits or two credits for a transaction
- recording different amounts for the debit and credit entries
- errors in transferring balances to the trial balance
- omission of a general ledger account in the trial balance

When errors are shown, the initial trial balance is 'balanced' by recording the difference in a suspense account, as shown in the Case Study below.

Case Study

SUSPENSE ACCOUNT

situation

The accounts assistant of Temeside Traders is unable to balance the initial trial balance on 31 December 20-4. As the error or errors cannot be found quickly, the trial balance is balanced by recording the difference in a suspense account:

	Dr	Cr
	£	£
Trial balance totals	100,000	99,700
Suspense account		300
	100,000	100,000

solution

A suspense account is opened in general ledger with, in this case, a credit balance of £300:

GENERAL LEDGER

Dr	Suspense Account		Cr
20-4	£	20-4	£
		31 Dec Trial balance difference	300

A detailed examination of the book-keeping system is now made in order to find the errors. As errors are found, they are corrected by means of a journal entry. The journal entries will balance, with one part of the entry being either a debit or credit to suspense account. In this way, the balance on suspense account will be eliminated by book-keeping transactions.

In the next section we will discuss how errors which are shown by a trial balance are corrected and will see an example journal entry for each.

ERRORS SHOWN BY THE TRIAL BALANCE: JOURNAL ENTRIES

We will now look at the journal entries needed to correct errors which are shown by a trial balance and present an example for each.

At the end of this section we will see how the suspense account from the Case Study above appears after the errors have been found and corrected on 4 January 20-5.

calculation errors in ledger accounts

Sales account was undercast (under-added) by £100 on 23 December 20-4.

As sales account was undercast, the correcting entry must credit sales account with £100. The correcting journal entry and ledger entry are:

Date	Details	Reference	Dr	Cr
20-5			£	£
4 Jan	Suspense	GL	100	
	Sales	GL		100
	Undercast on 23 December 20-4			
	now corrected			

GENERAL LEDGER

Dr   **Sales Account**   Cr

20-5	£	20-5		£
		4 Jan	Suspense	100

The entry in suspense account is shown on page 212.

single entry transactions

Telephone expenses of £55 were not recorded in the expenses account on 10 December 20-4.

As only the bank entry has been recorded, the correcting entry must complete double-entry book-keeping by debiting telephone expenses account with £55. The correcting journal entry and ledger entry are:

Date	Details	Reference	Dr	Cr
20-5			£	£
4 Jan	Telephone expenses	GL	55	
	Suspense	GL		55
	Omission of entry in expenses			
	account: paid from bank			
	on 10 December 20-4			

GENERAL LEDGER

Dr   **Telephone Expenses Account**   Cr

20-5		£	20-5	£
4 Jan	Suspense	55		

The entry in suspense account is shown on page 212.

recording two debits or two credits for a transaction

Stationery expenses of £48 were debited to both stationery account and bank account on 18 December 20-4.

As bank account has been debited in error with £48, the correcting journal entry must be in two parts to:

* remove the incorrect entry
* record the correct entry

Date	Details	Reference	Dr	Cr
20-5			£	£
4 Jan	Suspense	GL	48	
	Bank	CB		48
	Removing the incorrect entry:			
	payment for stationery expenses			
	debited to bank in error on			
	18 December 20-4			

Date	Details	Reference	Dr	Cr
20-5			£	£
4 Jan	Suspense	GL	48	
	Bank	CB		48
	Recording the correct entry:			
	payment for stationery expenses			
	debited to bank in error on			
	18 December 20-4			

GENERAL LEDGER

Dr		**Cash Book** (bank columns)		Cr
20-5	£	20-5		£
		4 Jan	Suspense	48
		4 Jan	Suspense	48

The entries in suspense account are shown on page 212.

recording different amounts for debit and credit entries

Payment made to A Wilson, a supplier, for £65 has been entered in bank account as £56 on 19 December 20-4.

As the credit entry in bank account has been entered incorrectly, the correcting journal entry must be in two parts to:

• remove the incorrect entry

• record the correct entry

Date	Details	Reference	Dr	Cr
20-5			£	£
4 Jan	Bank	CB	56	
	Suspense	GL		56
	Removing the incorrect entry:			
	payment to a supplier entered in			
	bank account as £56 instead of			
	£65 on 19 December 20-4			

Date	Details	Reference	Dr	Cr
20-5			£	£
4 Jan	Suspense	GL	65	
	Bank	CB		65
	Recording the correct entry:			
	payment to a supplier entered in			
	bank account as £56 instead of			
	£65 on 19 December 20-4			

GENERAL LEDGER

Dr		**Cash Book** (bank columns)		Cr
20-5		£	20-5	£
4 Jan	Suspense	56	4 Jan Suspense	65

The entries in suspense account are shown on page 212.

errors in transferring balances to the trial balance

The balance of rent account is £11,100 but it has been recorded in the trial balance as £11,000.

To correct this type of error needs a journal entry to take the wrong amount from suspense account and then to record the correct amount, ie a two-part journal entry. As rent account has a debit balance the journal entries are firstly to take out the wrong balance (debit suspense account and credit rent account in the trial balance) and then to record the correct balance (debit rent account in the trial balance and credit suspense account).

Date	Details	Reference	Dr	Cr
20-5			£	£
4 Jan	Suspense	GL	11,000	
	Removing the incorrect balance of			
	rent account from the trial balance			
	as at 31 December 20-4			

Date	Details	Reference	Dr	Cr
20-5			£	£
4 Jan	Suspense	GL		11,100
	Recording the correct balance of			
	rent account in the trial balance			
	as at 31 December 20-4			

Each of these journal entries is for a single transaction; the reason for this is because the account for rent is correct in general ledger and is not affected by the error of recording the wrong amount in the trial balance.

The entries in suspense account are shown on page 212.

Note that some businesses may have a policy of not recording journal entries to correct this type of error. As the ledger account balance is correct, policy might be to amend the incorrect balance and the balance of suspense account directly on the face of the trial balance.

omission of a general ledger account in the trial balance

Discount received account has been omitted from the trial balance. The balance of the account is £250 credit.

To correct this type of error needs a journal entry to record the balance which has been omitted. As this example omits an account with a credit balance we must record the inclusion of the account as debit suspense account and credit discount received account in the trial balance.

Date	Details	Reference	Dr	Cr
20-5			£	£
14 Jan	Suspense	GL	250	
	Recording the correct balance			
	of discount received account in			
	the trial balance as at			
	31 December 20-4			

This is a single entry transaction in the journal because the omitted account is correct in general ledger and is not affected by its omission in the trial balance. The entry in suspense account is shown below.

Note that some businesses may have a policy of correcting this type of error directly on the face of the trial balance without recording a journal entry.

suspense account

After these journal entries have been recorded in the general ledger accounts, suspense account appears as:

Dr			**Suspense Account**		Cr
20-5		£	20-4		£
4 Jan	Sales	100	31 Dec Trial balance difference		300
4 Jan	Bank	48	20-5		
4 Jan	Bank	48	4 Jan Telephone expenses		55
4 Jan	Bank	65	4 Jan Bank		56
4 Jan	Rent	11,000	4 Jan Rent		11,100
4 Jan	Discount received	250			
		11,511			11,511

Thus all the errors have been found, and suspense account now has a nil balance.

RE-DRAFTING THE TRIAL BALANCE

In the previous section we have seen how a suspense account is used to 'balance' an initial trial balance. The suspense account can have either a debit or a credit balance – it will depend on which of the columns of the initial trial balance is the lower amount. For example, from the Case Study on pages 206-207, the credit column of the trial balance was £300 less than the debit column: this means that £300 had to be credited to suspense account to 'balance' the trial balance.

Once a suspense account has been opened it is necessary to locate the errors in the accounting system – we have seen the six types of error that are revealed by a trial balance. When they have been found, the errors will be corrected by means of journal entries from which the ledgers will be updated. Correcting errors will have an effect on the trial balance and it is necessary to redraft the trial balance in order to show:

- that suspense account has been cleared
- the adjusted account balances

The Case Study which follows shows how an initial trial balance is redrafted to clear suspense account and adjust the account balances.

Case Study

REDRAFTING A TRIAL BALANCE

situation

On 30 June 20-6 Beacon Traders extracted an initial trial balance which did not balance, and a suspense account with a credit balance of £720 was opened.

On 1 July journal entries were prepared to correct the errors that had been found, and to clear the suspense account.

The list of balances in the initial trial balance, and the journal entries to correct the errors, are shown on the next page.

As the accounts assistant at Beacon Traders you are to redraft the trial balance by placing the figures in the debit or credit column. You take into account the journal entries to clear the suspense account.

Account name	Balances extracted on 30 June 20-6	Balances at 1 July 20-6	
	£	Debit £	Credit £
Vehicles	20,500		
Inventory (Stock)	11,945		
Bank overdraft	7,847		
Petty cash control	110		
Sales ledger control	28,368		
Purchases ledger control	12,591		
VAT owing to HM Revenue and Customs	2,084		
Capital	20,670		
Loan from bank	20,500		
Sales	84,567		
Sales returns	1,089		
Purchases	51,054		
Purchases returns	2,210		
Vehicle expenses	3,175		
Wages	22,864		
Rent and rates	8,210		
Advertising	2,174		
Heating and lighting	968		
Telephone	732		
Suspense account (credit balance)	720		
	Totals		

Journal entries

Account name	Debit £	Credit £
Suspense	225	
Bank		225
Suspense	225	
Bank		225

Account name	Debit £	Credit £
Sales	4,250	
Suspense		4,250
Suspense	4,520	
Sales		4,520

solution

The first thing you do is to check that the journal entries will clear the suspense account. You do this by writing up the suspense account from the journal entries as follows:

Dr			Suspense Account		Cr
20-6		£	20-6		£
1 Jul	Bank	225	30 Jun	Trial balance difference	720
1 Jul	Bank	225	1 Jul	Sales	4,250
1 Jul	Sales	4,520			
		4,970			4,970

Next you amend the account balances affected by the journal entries:

- bank overdraft

	£	
balance at 30 June 20-6	7,847	credit
suspense account	225	credit
suspense account	225	credit
revised balance at 1 July 20-6	8,297	credit

- sales

	£	
balance at 30 June 20-6	84,567	credit
suspense account	4,250	debit
suspense account	4,520	credit
revised balance at 1 July 20-6	84,837	credit

Lastly you redraft the trial balance, on the next page, which balances without using a suspense account. This shows that the accounting records are now arithmetically correct.

Account name	Balances extracted on 30 June 20-6	Balances at 1 July 20-6	
	£	Debit £	Credit £
Vehicles	20,500	20,500	
Inventory (Stock)	11,945	11,945	
Bank overdraft	7,847		8,297
Petty cash control	110	110	
Sales ledger control	28,368	28,368	
Purchases ledger control	12,591		12,591
VAT owing to HM Revenue & Customs	2,084		2,084
Capital	20,670		20,670
Loan from bank	20,500		20,500
Sales	84,567		84,837
Sales returns	1,089	1,089	
Purchases	51,054	51,054	
Purchases returns	2,210		2,210
Vehicle expenses	3,175	3,175	
Wages	22,864	22,864	
Rent and rates	8,210	8,210	
Advertising	2,174	2,174	
Heating and lighting	968	968	
Telephone	732	732	
Suspense account			–
Totals		151,189	151,189

Tutorial note: the accounts affected by the journal entries are bank, sales and suspense.

Chapter Summary

- Taking the balance of each account in general ledger, a trial balance can be extracted.

- A trial balance does not prove the complete accuracy of the accounting records as there may be:
  - errors not shown by a trial balance
  - errors shown by a trial balance

- Errors not shown by a trial balance are:
  - error of omission
  - error of commission
  - error of principle
  - error of original entry
  - reversal of entries
  - compensating error

- Errors shown by a trial balance are:
  - calculation errors in ledger accounts
  - single entry transactions
  - recording two debits or two credits for a transaction
  - recording different amounts for the debit and credit entries
  - errors in transferring balances to the trial balance
  - omission of a general ledger account in the trial balance

- Correction of errors is always a difficult topic to put into practice: it tests knowledge of double-entry book-keeping and it is all too easy to make the error worse than it was in the first place! The secret of correcting errors is to write down – in account format – what has gone wrong. It should then be relatively easy to see what has to be done to put the error right.

- All errors are non-regular transactions and need to be corrected by means of a journal entry: the book-keeper then records the correcting transactions in the accounts.

- When error(s) are shown by a trial balance, the amount of the error is placed in a suspense account. As the errors are found, journal entries are made which 'clear out' the suspense account.

Key Terms	**trial balance**	list of the balances of every account from general ledger (including cash book and petty cash book), distinguishing between those accounts which have debit balances and those which have credit balances
	error of omission	financial transaction completely omitted from the accounting records
	error of commission	transaction entered to the wrong person's account
	error of principle	transaction entered in the wrong type of account
	error of original entry	wrong amount entered incorrectly in accounts
	reversal of entries	debit and credit entries made on the wrong side of the accounts
	compensating error	where two errors cancel each other
	suspense account	account in which is placed the amount of an error shown by the initial trial balance, pending further investigation
	redrafted trial balance	trial balance which has been amended following correction of errors

Activities

10.1   The following errors have been made in the accounting records of Beacon Traders. Tick to show which of the errors below are, or are not, disclosed by the trial balance.

Error in the general ledger	Error disclosed by the trial balance	Error not disclosed by the trial balance
A bank payment for telephone expenses has been recorded on the debit side of both the cash book and telephone expenses account		
A payment recorded in bank account for vehicle repairs has been entered in vehicles account		
A sales invoice has been omitted from all accounting records		
The balance of purchases returns account has been calculated incorrectly		
A bank payment from a receivable (debtor) has been recorded in cash book and sales ledger only		
A bank payment of £85 for stationery has been recorded as £58 in both accounts		

10.2   An amount has been entered into the accounting system as £65 instead of £56. The error is called:

(a)   compensating error

(b)   error of commission

(c)   error of principle

(d)   error of original entry

Which one of these options is correct?

10.3 A trial balance failed to balance. The debit column totalled £154,896 and the credit column totalled £155,279. What entry would be made in the suspense account to balance the trial balance?

(a) £766 debit

(b) £383 debit

(c) £383 credit

(d) £766 credit

Which one of these options is correct?

10.4 A trial balance fails to agree by £75 and the difference is placed in a suspense account. Later it is found that a cash sale for this amount has not been entered in the sales account. Which one of the following journal entries is correct?

(a) debit suspense account £75; credit sales account £75

(b) debit suspense account £150; credit sales account £150

(c) debit sales account £75; credit suspense account £75

(d) credit sales account £75

Which one of these options is correct?

10.5 The following errors have been made in the general ledger of Mereford Manufacturing:

(a) £100 has been debited to rent account instead of to rates account.

(b) Sales returns have been entered into the accounting records as £96 instead of the correct amount of £69.

(c) Purchases returns of £175 have been debited to purchases returns account and credited to purchases ledger control account.

(d) Diesel fuel for vehicles of £45 has been debited to vehicles account.

You are to record the journal entries to correct the errors shown above in the general ledger (dates and narratives are not required).

10.6 The trial balance of Thomas Wilson balanced. However, a number of errors have been found in the accounting records:

(a) credit sale of £150 to J Rigby has not been entered in the accounts

(b) a bank payment for £125 to H Price Limited, a supplier, has been recorded in the account of H Prince

(c) the cost of a new delivery van, £10,000, has been entered to vehicle expenses account.

(d) postages of £55, paid by bank payment, have been entered on the wrong sides of both accounts

(e) both purchases account and purchases returns account have been undercast by £100

(f) a bank receipt for £89 from L Johnson, a customer, has been entered in the accounts as £98

You are to take each error in turn and:

- state the type of error

- show the correcting journal entry

10.7 The trial balance of Rose's Retail included a suspense account. All the book-keeping errors have now been traced and the journal entries shown below have been recorded.

Journal entries

Account name	Debit £	Credit £
Telephone expenses	210	
Suspense		210
Suspense	100	
Sales		100
Vehicle expenses	50	
Vehicles		50

As the accounts assistant at Rose's Retail you are to post the journal entries to the general ledger accounts. Dates are not required.

Telephone Expenses Account

Details	Amount £	Details	Amount £

Suspense Account

Details	Amount £	Details	Amount £
Balance b/d	110		

Sales Account

Details	Amount £	Details	Amount £

Vehicle Expenses Account

Details	Amount £	Details	Amount £

Vehicles Account

Details	Amount £	Details	Amount £

10.8 (a) The initial trial balance of Carrick Cards at 30 April 20-1 did not balance. The difference of £100 was placed into a suspense account.

The error has been traced to the sales day book as shown below.

Sales day book

Date 20-1	Details	Invoice number	Total £	VAT £	Net £
30 Apr	Bialas Ltd	4591	2,350	350	2,000
30 Apr	Corline and Co	4592	1,410	210	1,200
30 Apr	Thorpe Traders	4593	940	140	800
	Totals		4,700	600	4,000

As an accounts assistant at Carrick Cards you are to identify the error and record the journal entries needed for the general ledger to:

(i) remove the incorrect entry

(ii) record the correct entry

(iii) remove the suspense account balance

(i)

Account name	Amount £	Debit ✔	Credit ✔

(ii)

Account name	Amount £	Debit ✔	Credit ✔

(iii)

Account name	Amount £	Debit ✔	Credit ✔

(b)   A further error is discovered – a bank payment for vehicle expenses of £89 has been entered in the accounts as £98.

You are to record the journal entries needed for the general ledger to:

(i)   remove the incorrect entry

(ii)   record the correct entry

(i)

Account name	Amount £	Debit ✔	Credit ✔

(ii)

Account name	Amount £	Debit ✔	Credit ✔

10.9 Jeremy Johnson extracts a trial balance from his accounting records on 30 September 20-4. Unfortunately the trial balance fails to balance and the difference, £19 debit, is placed to a suspense account pending further investigation.

The following errors are later found:

(a)   a bank payment of £85 for office expenses has been entered in the bank account but no entry has been made in the office expenses account

(b)   a bank payment for photocopying of £87 has been correctly entered in the bank account, but is shown as £78 in the photocopying account

(c)   sales returns account has been overcast by £100

(d)   commission received of £25 has been entered twice in the account

You are to:

•   make journal entries to correct the errors

•   show the suspense account after the errors have been corrected

10.10 On 31 December 20-4 Chapelporth Supplies extracted an initial trial balance which did not balance, and a suspense account was opened. On 2 January 20-5 journal entries were prepared to correct the errors that had been found, and to clear the suspense account. The list of balances in the initial trial balance, and the journal entries to correct the errors, are shown on the next page.

As the accounts assistant at Chapelporth Supplies you are to redraft the trial balance by placing the figures in the debit or credit column. You should take into account the journal entries which will clear the suspense account.

Account name	Balances extracted on 31 December 20-4 £	Balances at 2 January 20-5	
		Debit £	Credit £
Office equipment	12,246		
Bank (debit balance)	3,091		
Petty cash control	84		
Inventory (Stock)	11,310		
Capital	18,246		
Loan from bank	8,290		
VAT owing to HM Revenue & Customs	3,105		
Purchases ledger control	17,386		
Sales ledger control	30,274		
Sales	82,410		
Purchases	39,996		
Purchases returns	2,216		
Sales returns	3,471		
Wages	20,212		
Advertising	4,300		
Insurance	1,045		
Heating and lighting	1,237		
Rent and rates	4,076		
Postages	721		
Suspense account (credit balance)	410		
	Totals		

Journal entries

Account name	Debit £	Credit £
Suspense	780	
Advertising		780
Advertising	870	
Suspense		870

Account name	Debit £	Credit £
Suspense	5,500	
Purchases		5,500
Purchases	5,000	
Suspense		5,000

10.11 On 30 April 20-8 Towanporth Traders extracted an initial trial balance which did not balance, and a suspense account was opened. On 1 May journal entries were prepared to correct the errors that had been found, and to clear the suspense account. The list of balances in the initial trial balance, and the journal entries to correct the errors, are shown below.

As the accounts assistant at Towanporth Traders you are to redraft the trial balance by placing the figures in the debit or credit column. You should take into account the journal entries which will clear the suspense account.

Account name	Balances extracted on 30 April 20-8 £	Balances at 1 May 20-8	
		Debit £	Credit £
Sales	101,169		
Sales returns	3,476		
Purchases	54,822		
Purchases returns	4,107		
Sales ledger control	25,624		
Purchases ledger control	18,792		
Rent and rates	3,985		
Advertising	4,867		
Insurance	1,733		
Wages	27,391		
Heating and lighting	3,085		
Miscellaneous expenses	107		
Capital	18,171		
Vehicles	22,400		
Inventory (Stock)	12,454		
Petty cash control	85		
Bank overdraft	6,041		
VAT owing to HM Revenue & Customs	3,054		
Loan from bank	12,200		
Suspense account (debit balance)	3,505		
	Totals		

Journal entries

Account name	Debit £	Credit £
Suspense	100	
Sales		100

Account name	Debit £	Credit £
Wages	3,855	
Suspense		3,855

Account name	Debit £	Credit £
Suspense	125	
Bank		125
Suspense	125	
Bank		125

Answers to activities

CHAPTER 1: INTRODUCTION TO BANKING PROCEDURES

1.1   (b)

1.2   False.

1.3   (c) and (f)

1.4   (b)

1.5   (a) 4, (b) 6, (c) 2.

1.6   False. The transaction will be refused if the money is not available.

1.7   (a)

1.8   (b)

1.9   (c)

1.10   (a)

1.11   (b)

1.12   (b)

1.13   (b)

1.14   (a) 6, (b) 1, (c) 3, (d) 4, (e) 2, (f) 5.

CHAPTER 2: RECEIVING AND RECORDING PAYMENTS

2.1	Customer	Change	Notes & coin given in change
	1	£1.50	1 x £1 coin, 1 x 50p coin
	2	£6.70	1 x £5 note, 1 x £1 coin, 1 x 50p coin, 1 x 20p coin
	3	£2.49	1 x £2 coin, 2 x 20p coins, 1 x 5p coin, 2 x 2p coins
	4	£3.21	1 x £2 coin, 1 x £1 coin, 1 x 20p coin, 1 x 1p coin
	5	£0.66	1 x 50p coin, 1 x 10p coin, 1 x 5p coin, 1 x 1p coin
	6	£3.78	1 x £2 coin, 1 x £1 coin, 1 x 50p coin, 1 x 20p coin, 1 x 5p coin, 1 x 2p coin, 1 x 1p coin
	7	£7.24	1 x £5 note, 1 x £2 coin, 1 x 20p coin, 2 x 2p coins
	8	£0.58	1 x 50p coin, 1 x 5p coin, 1 x 2p coin, 1 x 1p coin
	9	£3.46	1 x £2 coin, 1 x £1 coin, 2 x 20p coins, 1 x 5p coin, 1 x 1p coin
	10	£1.92	1 x £1 coin, 1 x 50p coin, 2 x 20p coins, 1 x 2p coin

2.2

	£
cash float at start of day	28.71
plus sales made during the day	46.46
equals amount of cash held at end of day	75.17

2.3 (a) 2 x £13.99 = £27.98; 2 x 85p = £1.70; total £29.68 + VAT £5.19 = £34.87

(b) £149.95 + 99p = £150.94; add VAT of £26.41 = £177.35

(c) 2 x £35.99 = £71.98; add VAT of £12.59 = £84.57

2.4 (a) Payee name incorrect, cheque out of date, cheque not signed, amount in words and figures differs

(b) Amount in words and figures differs

(c) Out of date, amount in words and figures differs

2.5 (c)

2.6 (d)

2.7 (b)

2.8 (a)

2.9 Encryption is a method of encoding data so that payment details, eg card numbers, security codes, expiry dates – should remain secret and unavailable to hackers. The padlock symbol is displayed in sites to let customers know that sensitive data will be encrypted.

2.10 A remittance advice is a document sent to a supplier advising that money is being sent, either using a cheque (which will accompany the advice) or a BACS payment made direct to the supplier's bank account.

A remittance list is a record of items received through the post or over the counter. It is likely to include columns for the date, sender, the nature of the 'remittance' amount and the signature of the person opening the post.

CHAPTER 3: PAYING INTO THE BANK

3.1   (c)

3.2   Cheques:

Cheques:		Cash:		
	£20.00	Cash:	2 x £20 notes	£40.00
	£18.50		5 x £10 notes	£50.00
	£75.25		8 x £5 notes	£40.00
	<u>£68.95</u>		2 x £1 coins	£2.00
	£182.70		6 x 50p coins	£3.00
			4 x 10p coins	£0.40
			2 x 2p coins	<u>£0.04</u>
				£135.44

Total amount of credit: £318.14.

3.3   Total of sales vouchers £396.94 less refund voucher £13.50, total of summary £383.44.

3.4   (a)   £2,678.90 at the beginning, £5,959.43 at the end.

(b)   3 giro credits on 10, 13, 17 November, total £1,595.30.

(c)   5 cheques on 10, 11, 21, 24, 27 November, total £1,632.27.

(d)   BACS direct credits from customers.

(e)   25 Nov Ion Power £167.50, 27 November Mercury Telecom £96.50.

(f)   £3,006.70 on 24 November through Netsales.

(g)   'DR' is short for 'debit' which in banking terms means an overdraft (the customer borrowing). If this has been the case the bank balance during the month would have gone into credit, ending up with a balance of £601.63 CR.

CHAPTER 4: MAKING PAYMENTS

4.1   False. No cheque is involved in a BACS payment.

4.2   For security reasons: to prevent fraudulent alterations.

4.3   (d)

4.4   To establish the legal relationship between the bank and the business. The bank has to know *who* can sign cheques, and for what amounts. It also needs specimen signatures so that it can verify written instructions, eg cheque signatures and other payment instructions.

4.5   (a)   See text pages 64 and 67.   (b) Standing order   (c) Direct debit

4.6   (a)   Bank draft   (b) CHAPS

4.7   (a)   He/she doesn't have to rely on carrying his/her own money; <u>or</u> he/she doesn't have to pay!

(b)   Monitoring of expenditure, <u>or</u> control of expenditure.

4.8   Note that the cash discount is not available – the period has expired. Total £15,255.34.

4.9   Total £4,083.05.

4.10   The most <u>normal</u> methods would be:
(a)   BACS
(b)   bank giro credit
(c)   bank draft
(d)   company credit card
(e)   CHAPS

4.11   **standing order**

(a)   Standing order completed as shown below.

(b)   The form will be sent to the National Bank, as they will set up the payments.

(c)   The standing order will have to be signed by an authorised signatory (or two) within the business. It should also be noted that details of the due payments will be passed to the person in charge of entering up the cash book as the payments will form part of the double-entry book-keeping of the company.

STANDING ORDER MANDATE

To _____ *NATIONAL* _____ Bank

Address _____ *10 CATHEDRAL STREET MEREFORD MR1 5DE* _____

PLEASE PAY TO

Bank _*BARCLAYS*_   Branch _*EVESHORE*_   Sort code | *30 98 15* |

Beneficiary _____   Account number | *726 271 61* |

The sum of £ *350*   Amount in words *THREE HUNDRED AND FIFTY POUNDS*

Date of first payment *15 MAY 2003*   Frequency of payment *MONTHLY*

Until *15 APRIL 2004*   Reference *BE/ 6637*

Account to be debited *NIMROD DRAINAGE LTD*   Account number *1203 4875*

SIGNATURE(S) ....

.... date................

direct debit

(a)   Direct debit form completed as shown below (standing order form above).

(b)   The form will be sent to Tradesure Insurance, as they will set up the payments.

(c)   The direct debit will have to be signed by an authorised signatory (or two) within the business. It should also be noted that details of the due payments are normally advised by the originator of the direct debit (here the insurance company). These will be passed to the person in charge of entering up the cash book as the payments will form part of the double-entry book-keeping of the company.

—————— direct debit instruction ——————

Tradesure Insurance Company
PO Box 134, Helliford, HL9 6TY

Originator's Identification Number 914208
03924540234

Reference(tobecompletedbyTradesureInsurance)..........................

Please complete the details and return this form to Tradesure Insurance

name and address of bank/building society

_ _ *NATIONAL   BANK* _ _ _ _ _
_ _ *10   CATHEDRAL   STREET* _ _ _
_ _ *MEREFORD* _ _ _ _ _ _ _ _ _
MR1 5DE

account name
NIMROD DRAINAGE LIMITED

account number   sort code
1203 4875   *35.09.75*

instructions to bank/building society

- I instruct you to pay direct debits from my account at the request of Tradesure Insurance Company
- The amounts are variable and may be debited on various dates
- I understand that Tradesure Insurance Company may change the amounts and dates only after giving me prior notice
- I will inform the bank/building society if I wish to cancel this instruction
- I understand that if any direct debit is paid which breaks the terms of this instruction, the bank/building society will make a refund.

signature(s)   date

CHAPTER 5: CASH BOOK

5.1 (c)

5.2 (a)

5.3

			True	False
	(a)	Cash book is the book of prime entry for bank and cash receipts and payments	✔	
	(b)	Cash book can be the double-entry account for bank and cash	✔	
	(c)	The discount received column total from cash book is debited to discount received account in general ledger		✔
	(d)	The VAT column total on the receipts side of cash book is debited to VAT account in general ledger		✔
	(e)	The sales ledger column total from cash book is credited to sales ledger control account in general ledger	✔	

5.4 (a)

Dr   **Cash Book**   Cr

Date	Details	Ref	Discount allowed	Cash	Bank	Date	Details	Ref	Discount received	Cash	Bank
20-2			£	£	£	20-2			£	£	£
1 Jun	Balance b/d			280		1 Jun	Balance b/d				2,240
3 Jun	G Wheaton		5	195		8 Jun	F Lloyd		10		390
5 Jun	T Francis		2	53		10 Jun	Wages			165	
16 Jun	Bank	C		200		12 Jun	A Morris		3	97	
18 Jun	H Watson		30		640	16 Jun	Cash	C			200
28 Jun	M Perry		6		234	20 Jun	R Marks				78
30 Jun	K Willis			45		24 Jun	D Farr		2		65
30 Jun	Balance c/d				1,904	26 Jun	Telephone			105	
						30 Jun	Balance c/d			211	
			43	578	2,973				15	578	2,973
1 Jul	Balance b/d			211		1 Jul	Balance b/d				1,904

(b)

GENERAL LEDGER

Dr	**Discount Allowed Account**		Cr
20-2	£	20-2	£
30 Jun Cash Book	43		

Dr	**Discount Received Account**		Cr
20-2		£ 20-2	£
		30 Jun Cash Book	15

5.5   (a) – (c)

Dr											Cr
					Cash Book						
Date	Details	Ref	Discount allowed	Cash	Bank	Date	Details	Ref	Discount received	Cash	Bank
20-7			£	£	£	20-7			£	£	£
1 Aug	Balances b/d			276	4,928	5 Aug	T Hall Ltd		24		541
1 Aug	Wild & Sons Ltd				398	8 Aug	Wages			254	
11 Aug	Bank	C		500		11 Aug	Cash	C			500
12 Aug	A Lewis Ltd			20	1,755	18 Aug	F Jarvis				457
21 Aug	Harvey & Sons Ltd				261	22 Aug	Wages			436	
29 Aug	Wild & Sons Ltd			15	595	25 Aug	J Jones		33		628
29 Aug	Bank	C		275		27 Aug	Salaries				2,043
						28 Aug	Telephone				276
						29 Aug	Cash	C			275
						31 Aug	Balances c/d			361	3,217
			35	1,051	7,937				57	1,051	7,937
1 Jul	Balances b/d			361	3,217						

(d)

GENERAL LEDGER

Dr	**Discount Allowed Account**		Cr
20-7	£	20-7	£
31 Aug Cash Book	35		

Dr		**Discount Received Account**			Cr
20-7		£	20-7		£
			31 Aug Cash Book		57

(e)

SALES LEDGER

Dr		**Wild & Sons Ltd**			Cr
20-7		£	20-7		£
			29 Aug Discount allowed		15

Dr		**A Lewis Ltd**			Cr
20-7		£	20-7		£
			12 Aug Discount allowed		20

(f)

PURCHASES LEDGER

Dr		**T Hall Ltd**			Cr
20-7		£	20-7		£
5 Aug Discount received		24			

Dr		**J Jones**			Cr
20-7		£	20-7		£
25 Aug Discount received		33			

5.6 (a) – (b)

Dr (Receipts)

Date	Details	Ref	Discount allowed	Cash	Bank	VAT	Cash sales	Sales ledger	Other receipts
20-7			£	£	£	£	£	£	£
12 May	Balances b/d			205.75	825.30				
12 May	Sales	GL			534.62	79.62	455.00		
13 May	Sales	GL		164.50		24.50	140.00		
13 May	T Jarvis	SL	2.50		155.00			155.00	
14 May	Sales	GL			752.00	112.00	640.00		
15 May	Cash	C			250.00				
15 May	Sales	GL		264.37		39.37	225.00		
16 May	Wyvern Council	SL	5.00		560.45			560.45	
			7.50	634.62	3,077.37	255.49	1,460.00	715.45	–

Cr (Payments)

Date	Details	Ref	Discount received	Cash	Bank	VAT	Cash purchases	Purchases ledger	Other payments
			£	£	£	£	£	£	£
20-7									
12 May	Rent	GL			255.50				255.50
13 May	Terry Carpets	PL	4.65		363.55			363.55	
14 May	Trade Supplies	PL	3.50		145.50			145.50	
14 May	Purchases	GL		28.20		4.20	24.00		
15 May	Bank	C		250.00					
15 May	Longlife Carpets	PL	4.30		291.50			291.50	
16 May	Purchases	GL			258.50	38.50	220.00		
16 May	Balances c/d			356.42	1,762.82				
			12.45	634.62	3,077.37	42.70	244.00	800.55	255.50

(c) Transfers to general ledger:

- *discount allowed* column total of £7.50 is debited to discount allowed account and credited to sales ledger control account

- *discount received* column total of £12.45 is credited to discount received account and debited to purchases ledger control account

(d)

SALES LEDGER

Dr	**T Jarvis**				Cr
20-7	£	20-7			£
		13 May	Discount allowed	GL	2.50

Dr	**Wyvern Council**				Cr
20-7	£	20-7			£
		16 May	Discount allowed	GL	5.00

PURCHASES LEDGER

Dr	**Terry Carpets**		Cr
20-7	£	20-7	£
13 May Discount received GL	4.65		

Dr	**Trade Supplies**		Cr
20-7	£	20-7	£
14 May Discount received GL	3.50		

Dr	**Longlife Carpets**		Cr
20-7	£	20-7	£
15 May Discount received GL	4.30		

CHAPTER 6: BANK RECONCILIATION STATEMENTS

6.1 (a)

6.2 (c)

6.3

> **TOM REID**
> **BANK RECONCILIATION STATEMENT AS AT 31 DECEMBER 20-2**
>
> | | £ |
> |---|---|
> | Balance at bank as per bank statement | 207 |
> | *Less:* unpresented cheque: | |
> | B Kay (cheque no 345126) | 20 |
> | | 187 |
> | *Add:* outstanding lodgement: | |
> | J Hill | 13 |
> | Balance at bank as per cash book | 200 |

6.4 (a)

Cash Book (bank columns)

20-3	Receipts		£	20-3	Payments		£
1 Jan	Balance b/d		800.50	2 Jan	A Arthur Ltd	001351	100.00
6 Jan	J Baker		495.60	9 Jan	C Curtis	001352	398.50
30 Jan	G Shotton Ltd		335.75	13 Jan	Donald & Co	001353	229.70
13 Jan	TK Supplies	BACS	716.50	14 Jan	Bryant & Sons	001354	312.00
				23 Jan	P Reid	001355	176.50
				23 Jan	Omni Finance	DD	207.95
				31 Jan	Balance c/d		923.70
			2,348.35				2,348.35
1 Feb	Balance b/d		923.70				

(b)

> **P GERRARD**
> **BANK RECONCILIATION STATEMENT AS AT 31 JANUARY 20-3**
>
> | | £ | £ |
> |---|---|---|
> | Balance at bank as per bank statement | | 1,076.45 |
> | *Less:* unpresented cheques: | | |
> | Bryant & Sons (001354) | 312.00 | |
> | P Reid (001355) | 176.50 | |
> | | | 488.50 |
> | | | 587.95 |
> | *Add:* outstanding lodgement: | | |
> | G Shotton Limited | | 335.75 |
> | Balance at bank as per cash book | | 923.70 |

6.5 (a)

Cash Book (bank columns)

20-4	Receipts	£	20-4	Payments		£
1 May	Balance b/d	300	3 May	P Stone	867714	28
7 May	Cash	162	14 May	Alpha Ltd	867715	50
17 May	C Brewster	89	28 May	E Deakin	867716	110
24 May	Cash	60	17 May	Standing order: A-Z Insurance		25
28 May	Cash	40	31 May	Bank charges		10
			31 May	Balance c/d		428
		651				651
1 Jun	Balance b/d	428				

(b)

JANE DOYLE

BANK RECONCILIATION STATEMENT AS AT 31 MAY 20-4

	£
Balance at bank as per bank statement	498
Less: unpresented cheque:	
E Deakin (867716)	110
	388
Add: outstanding lodgement:	
cash	40
Balance at bank as per cash book	428

6.6 (a) - (c)

CASH BOOK

Date	Details	Bank	Date	Cheque no	Details	Bank
20-5		£	20-5			£
1 May	Balance b/f	3,652	4 May	451762	Smith and Company	751
26 May	J Ackland	832	4 May	451763	Bryant Limited	268
28 May	Stamp Limited	1,119	7 May	451764	Curtis Cars	1,895
14 May	Perran Taxis	2,596	7 May	451765	Parts Supplies	1,045
			18 May		Wyvern Council	198
			20 May		A1 Insurance	1,005
			25 May		Okaro and Company	254
			25 May		Bank charges	20
			31 May		Balance c/d	2,763
		8,199				8,199
1 Jun	Balance b/d	2,763				

(d)

MILESTONE MOTORS

Bank Reconciliation Statement as at 31 May 20-5

	£	£
Balance at bank as per bank statement		2,707
Less: unpresented cheque no 451764		1,895
		812
Add: outstanding lodgements		
J Ackland	832	
Stamp Limited	1,119	
		1,951
Balance at bank as per cash book		2,763

6.7 (a) – (c)

CASH BOOK

Date	Details	Bank	Date	Cheque no	Details	Bank
20-8		£	20-8			£
1 Jun	Balance b/f	1,890	1 Jun	364125	Penryn Ltd	427
20 Jun	Chiverton Ltd	1,200	3 Jun	364126	Fal Boats	760
24 Jun	Perran Ltd	4,750	10 Jun	364127	S Mawes	4,200
24 Jun	P Porth	8,950	20 Jun	364128	Castle Supplies	1,062
24 Jun	Sand & Stone	2,486	21 Jun		J C Property Co	850
25 Jun	Surfrider Ltd	4,110	25 Jun		Vord Finance	275
			27 Jun		Balance c/d	15,812
		23,386				23,386
28 Jun	Balance b/d	15,812				

(d)

Bank reconciliation statement as at 27 June 20-8	
Balance as per bank statement	£ 1,672
Add	
Name: Chiverton Ltd	£ 1,200
Name: Perran Ltd	£ 4,750
Name: P Porth	£ 8,950
Name:	£
Total to add	£ 14,900
Less	
Name: Fal Boats 364126	£ 760
Name:	£
Name:	£
Name:	£
Total to subtract	£ 760
Balance as per cash book	£ 15,812

CHAPTER 7: PETTY CASH BOOK

7.1   (d)

7.2   *Allow:* (a), (b), (f), (g), (h), (j) – all supported by an appropriate receipt being attached to the petty cash voucher.

Refer:

(c)   travel to work – not normally a business expense, except for emergency call-outs

(d)   donation to charity – subject to authorisation by supervisor

(e)   staff tea and coffee – check if it is company policy to pay for this personal expense of the office staff

(i)   shelving for the office – this expense is too large to be paid out of petty cash; instead it should be referred to the accounts supervisor, who may authorise it for payment from the cash book by the cashier.

7.3

petty cash voucher		number 851		
		date *today*		
description			amount	
			£	p
Postage on a recorded delivery letter to			4	45
Evelode Supplies Ltd				
			4	45
	VAT at 17.5%			
			4	45
signature	*Jayne Smith*			
authorised	*A Student*			

Documentation will be a Post Office receipt for £4.45.

petty cash voucher			number 852	
			date *today*	
description			amount	
			£	p
Airmail envelopes			2	00
			2	00
		VAT at 17.5%	0	35
			2	35
signature	Tanya Howard			
authorised	A Student			

Documentation will be a till receipt from the stationery shop for £2.35.

petty cash voucher			number 853	
			date *today*	
description			amount	
			£	p
Taxi fare re visit to Jasper Ltd			7	32
			7	32
		VAT at 17.5%	1	28
			8	60
signature	Josh Delabole			
authorised	A Student			

Documentation will be a receipt from the taxi company for £8.60.

7.4

	Expense (excluding VAT) £	VAT £	Total £
(a)	8.00	1.40	9.40
(b)	4.00	0.70	4.70
(c)	2.00	0.35	2.35
(d)	2.09	0.36	2.45
(e)	4.77	0.83	5.60
(f)	2.96	0.51	3.47
(g)	7.45	1.30	8.75
(h)	0.80	0.14	0.94
(i)	0.85	0.14	0.99
(j)	8.01	1.40	9.41

7.5

					Petty Cash Book				**PCB55**
Receipts	Date	Details	Voucher number	Total payment	Analysis columns				
					VAT	Postages	Travel	Meals	Office sundries
£	20-2			£	£	£	£	£	£
100.00	1 Aug	Balance b/d							
	4 Aug	Postages	323	10.20		10.20			
	6 Aug	Travel expenses	324	8.50			8.50		
	9 Aug	Postages	325	5.60		5.60			
	12 Aug	Envelopes	326	9.40	1.40				8.00
	13 Aug	Window cleaning	327	14.10	2.10				12.00
	17 Aug	Taxi fare	328	11.75	1.75		10.00		
	20 Aug	Postages	329	9.40		9.40			
	23 Aug	Meals	330	12.20				12.20	
	27 Aug	Envelopes	331	7.52	1.12				6.40
				88.67	6.37	25.20	18.50	12.20	26.40
88.67	31 Aug	Bank							
	31 Aug	Balance c/d		100.00					
188.67				188.67					
100.00	1 Sep	Balance b/d							

7.6

					Petty Cash Book					**PCB42**	

Receipts	Date	Details	Voucher number	Total payment	\multicolumn{6}{c}{Analysis columns}					
					VAT	Travel	Postages	Stationery	Meals	Misc
£	20-3			£	£	£	£	£	£	£
150.00	1 Aug	Balance b/d								
	4 Aug	Taxi fare	39	9.40	1.40	8.00				
	6 Aug	Postage	40	5.50			5.50			
	9 Aug	Marker pens	41	3.76	0.56			3.20		
	11 Aug	Travel expenses	42	10.50		10.50				
	12 Aug	Window cleaner	43	14.10	2.10					12.00
	16 Aug	Envelopes	44	4.70	0.70			4.00		
	18 Aug	Donation	45	10.00						10.00
	19 Aug	Rail fare/meal allow	46	16.60		10.60			6.00	
	20 Aug	Postage	47	2.30			2.30			
	23 Aug	Tape	48	2.35	0.35			2.00		
	25 Aug	Postage	49	1.50			1.50			
	27 Aug	Taxi fare	50	14.10	2.10	12.00				
				94.81	7.21	41.10	9.30	9.20	6.00	22.00
94.81	31 Aug	Bank								
	31 Aug	Balance c/d		150.00						
244.81				244.81						
150.00	1 Sep	Balance b/d								

7.7 (a)

Total of petty cash payments for June		£56.72
Cash remaining should be		£93.28
Actual cash remaining is:		

	as at 30 June	
	number held	value (£)
£10 notes	3	30.00
£5 notes	8	40.00
£1 coins	15	15.00
50p coins	11	5.50
20p coins	6	1.20
10p coins	11	1.10
5p coins	5	0.25
2p coins	6	0.12
1p coins	11	0.11
TOTAL		93.28
Amount of discrepancy (if any)		£ nil

(b) If there is a discrepancy – whether a shortfall or a surplus – it should be investigated promptly and, if it cannot be resolved, should be referred to the accounts supervisor.

7.8 (a) and (b)

					Analysis columns				
Receipts	Date	Details	Voucher number	Total payment	VAT	Postages	Travel	Meals	Sundry office
£	20-4			£	£	£	£	£	£
150.00	7 Jun	Balance b/d							
	7 Jun	Postages	123	6.35		6.35			
	8 Jun	Travel expenses	124	8.25			8.25		
	8 Jun	Postages	125	3.28		3.28			
	9 Jun	Envelopes	126	4.70	0.70				4.00
	9 Jun	Window cleaning	127	14.10	2.10				12.00
	10 Jun	Taxi fare/meals	128	21.15	3.15		6.00	12.00	
	10 Jun	Postages/envelopes	129	14.14	0.84	8.50			4.80
	10 Jun	Taxi fare/meals	130	23.50	3.50		12.00	8.00	
	11 Jun	Pens/envelopes	131	7.52	1.12				6.40
				102.99	11.41	18.13	26.25	20.00	27.20
102.99	11 Jun	Bank							
	11 Jun	Balance c/d		150.00					
252.99				252.99					
150.00	12 Jun	Balance b/d							

Petty Cash Book — PCB18

(c)

GENERAL LEDGER

Petty Cash Control Account

Dr		£				Cr £
20-4			20-4			
7 Jun	Balance b/d	150.00	11 Jun	Petty cash book PCB18		102.99
11 Jun	Bank	102.99	11 Jun	Balance c/d		150.00
		252.99				252.99
12 Jun	Balance b/d	150.00				

CHAPTER 8: USING CONTROL ACCOUNTS

8.1 (b)

8.2

Dr		Sales Ledger Control Account			Cr
20-7		£	20-7		£
1 Jun	Balance b/d	17,491	30 Jun	Sales returns	1,045
30 Jun	Sales	42,591	30 Jun	Bank	39,024
			30 Jun	Balance c/d	20,013
		60,082			60,082
1 Jul	Balance b/d	20,013			

8.3 (a)

Sales Ledger Control Account

Date 20-5	Details	Amount £	Date 20-5	Details	Amount £
1 Jun	Balance b/d	180,824	30 Jun	Bank	96,214
30 Jun	Sales	118,600	30 Jun	Discounts allowed	300
			30 Jun	Sales returns	650
			30 Jun	Bad debt	350
			30 Jun	Balance c/d	201,910
		299,424			299,424
1 Jul	Balance b/d	201,910			

(b)

	£
Sales ledger control account balance as at 30 June 20-5	201,910
Total of sales ledger accounts as at 30 June 20-5	202,260
Difference	350

(c)   The bad debt of £350 may not have been written off in the sales ledger, and could relate to the account of Brandon Limited.

8.4   (a)   **Sales ledger control account**

	Amount	Debit	Credit
	£	✔	✔
Balance of receivables at 1 September 20-2	47,238	✔	
Goods sold on credit	31,054	✔	
Money received from receivables	29,179		✔
Goods returned by receivables	2,684		✔
Discounts allowed	784		✔
Bad debt written off	450		✔

(b)

£45,195	✔

(c)

£467, ie £45,195 (sales ledger control account) – £44,728 (sales ledger)

(d)

Money received from customers has been overstated in the sales ledger	✔
Sales to credit customers have been understated in the sales ledger	✔

8.5

	no action ✔	letter/email ✔	letter/email + phone call ✔
Benn Ltd		✔	
Charteris & Co	✔		
D Morgan	✔		
Wilson & Sons			✔

8.6 (c)

8.7

Dr   **Purchases Ledger Control Account**   Cr

20-9		£	20-9		£
30 Apr	Purchases returns	653	1 Apr	Balance b/d	14,275
30 Apr	Bank	31,074	30 Apr	Purchases	36,592
30 Apr	Set-off: sales ledger	597			
30 Apr	Balance c/d	18,543			
		50,867			50,867
			1 May	Balance b/d	18,543

8.8 (a)

Purchases Ledger Control Account

Date 20-3	Details	Amount £	Date 20-3	Details	Amount £
31 May	Bank	13,750	1 May	Balance b/d	50,300
31 May	Discounts received	500	31 May	Purchases	21,587
31 May	Purchases returns	250			
31 May	Balance c/d	57,387			
		71,887			71,887
			1 Jun	Balance b/d	57,387

(b)

	£
Purchases ledger control account balance as at 31 May 20-3	57,387
Total of purchases ledger accounts as at 31 May 20-3	56,387
Difference	1,000

(c)   There may have been a posting error and the debit balance of £500 for PP Properties may in fact be a credit balance.

8.9   (a)   **Purchases ledger control account**

	Amount	Debit	Credit
	£	✔	✔
Balance of creditors at 1 August 20-4	46,297		✔
Purchases from credit suppliers	22,084		✔
Payments made to credit suppliers	25,934	✔	
Discounts received	425	✔	
Goods returned to credit suppliers	1,108	✔	

(b)

£40,914	✔

(c)   £

Balance on purchases ledger control account at 1 September 20-4	40,914
Total of the purchases ledger balances at 1 September 20-4	39,906
Difference	1,008

(d)

A credit note was not entered in the purchases ledger control account	✔

8.10

	debit ✔	credit ✔
VAT on credit purchases	✔	
VAT on cash sales		✔
VAT on purchases returns		✔
VAT on credit sales		✔
VAT on sales returns	✔	

8.11   (a) and (b)

VAT Control Account

Date 20-4	Details	Amount £	Date 20-4	Details	Amount £
30 Jun	Purchases	4,060	30 Jun	Sales	9,800
30 Jun	Sales returns	252	30 Jun	Purchases returns	196
30 Jun	Balance c/d	6,118	30 Jun	Cash sales	434
		10,430			10,430
			1 Jul	Balance b/d	6,118

(c)   Is the VAT return correct? No

Reason: It is likely that the VAT on sales returns has been omitted from the VAT return. The correct amount owing to HM Revenue and Customs is £6,118.

CHAPTER 9: THE JOURNAL

9.1   (c)

9.2   (b)

9.3   *financial transaction*
- opening entries for a new business
- credit purchase of goods from a supplier
- returned credit purchases to the supplier
- customer returns goods sold on credit
- BACS receipt from a customer
- credit sale of goods to a customer
- expense paid out of petty cash

book of prime entry
- journal
- purchases day book
- purchases returns day book
- sales returns day book
- cash book
- sales day book
- petty cash book

9.4

Date	Details	Reference	Dr	Cr
			£	£
20-8				
1 May	Vehicle	GL	6,500	
	Fixtures and fittings	GL	2,800	
	Inventory (Stock)	GL	4,100	
	Bank	CB	150	
	Loan from husband	GL		5,000
	Capital*	GL		8,550
			13,550	13,550
	Assets and liabilities at the start of business			

* Assets – liabilities = capital (6,500 + 2,800 + 4,100 + 150 – 5,000 = 8,550)

9.5

Account name	Amount	Debit	Credit
	£	✔	✔
Cash	200	✔	
Cash at bank	2,340	✔	
Capital	9,874		✔
Payables	3,985		✔
Receivables	4,751	✔	
Loan from bank	12,650		✔
Office equipment	4,120	✔	
Rent paid	950	✔	
Inventory (Stock)	2,310	✔	
Sundry expenses	1,194	✔	
Vehicles	8,350	✔	
Wages	2,294	✔	

Opening capital = £9,874 (assets £26,509 – liabilities £16,635)

9.6   (d)

9.7

Account name	Amount	Debit	Credit
	£	✔	✔
Bad debts	840	✔	
VAT	147	✔	
Sales ledger control	987		✔

9.8 (d)

9.9 (c)

9.10 (a)

9.11 (a)   £111,650, ie £101,500 + £10,150

(b)   £40,510, ie £20,500 + £9,860 + £10,150

(c)   £70,290, ie £101,500 − £20,500 − £9,860 − £850

(d)

JOURNAL

Date	Details	Reference	Dr	Cr
20-3			£	£
31 Oct	Wages expense		111,650	
	Wages control			111,650
	Transfer of wages expense			

Date	Details	Reference	Dr	Cr
20-3			£	£
31 Oct	Wages control		40,510	
	HM Revenue & Customs			40,510
	Amount due to HMRC			

Date	Details	Reference	Dr	Cr
20-3			£	£
31 Oct	Wages control		70,290	
	Bank			70,290
	Net wages paid to employees			

Date	Details	Reference	Dr	Cr
20-3			£	£
31 Oct	Wages control		850	
	Trade union fees			850
	Amount due for trade union fees			

9.12 (a)

Account name	Amount £	Debit ✔	Credit ✔
Wages expense	56,110	✔	
Wages control	56,110		✔

(b)

Account name	Amount £	Debit ✔	Credit ✔
Wages control	21,105	✔	
HM Revenue & Customs	21,105		✔

(c)

Account name	Amount £	Debit ✔	Credit ✔
Wages control	32,805	✔	
Bank	32,805		✔

(d)

Account name	Amount £	Debit ✔	Credit ✔
Wages control	2,200	✔	
Pension fund	2,200		✔

CHAPTER 10: THE TRIAL BALANCE AND CORRECTION OF ERRORS

10.1

Error in the general ledger	Error disclosed by the trial balance	Error not disclosed by the trial balance
A bank payment for telephone expenses has been recorded on the debit side of both the cash book and telephone expenses account	✔	
A payment recorded in bank account for vehicle repairs has been entered in vehicles account		✔
A sales invoice has been omitted from all accounting records		✔
The balance of purchases returns account has been calculated incorrectly	✔	
A bank payment from a receivable (debtor) has been recorded in cash book and sales ledger only	✔	
A bank payment of £85 for stationery has been recorded as £58 in both accounts		✔

10.2 (d)

10.3 (b)

10.4 (a)

10.5

Date	Details	Reference	Dr	Cr
			£	£
(a)	Rates	GL	100	
	Rent	GL		100
(b)	Sales ledger control	GL	96	
	Sales returns	GL		96
	Sales returns	GL	69	
	Sales ledger control	GL		69

Date	Details	Reference	Dr	Cr
			£	£
(c)	Purchases ledger control	GL	175	
	Purchases returns	GL		175
	Purchases ledger control	GL	175	
	Purchases returns	GL		175
(d)	Vehicle running expenses	GL	45	
	Vehicles	GL		45

Tutorial note: for errors (b) and (c) two journal entries are required – firstly to remove the incorrect entry and, secondly, to record the correct entry.

10.6 (a) *error of omission*

Date	Details	Reference	Dr	Cr
			£	£
	Sales ledger control	GL	150	
	Sales	GL		150
	Invoice no .... omitted from the accounts: in the sales ledger – debit J Rigby £150			

(b) *error of commission*

Date	Details	Reference	Dr	Cr
			£	£
	Purchases ledger control	GL	125	
	Purchases ledger control	GL		125
	Correction of error (bank payment no ... in the purchases ledger – debit H Price Limited £125 – credit H Prince £125			

(c) *error of principle*

Date	Details	Reference	Dr	Cr
			£	£
	Delivery van	GL	10,000	
	Vehicle expenses	GL		10,000
	Correction of error – vehicle no .... invoice no .... debited to vehicle expenses in error			

(d)   *reversal of entries*

Date	Details	Reference	Dr	Cr
			£	£
	Postages	GL	55	
	Bank	CB		55
	Removing the incorrect entry: bank payment on ...(date)... for postages entered on the wrong side of both accounts			

Date	Details	Reference	Dr	Cr
			£	£
	Postages	GL	55	
	Bank	CB		55
	Recording the correct entry: bank payment on ...(date)... for postages entered on the wrong side of both accounts			

(e)   *compensating error*

Date	Details	Reference	Dr	Cr
			£	£
	Purchases	GL	100	
	Purchases returns	GL		100
	Correction of undercast on purchases account and purchases returns account on ...(date)...			

(f)   *error of original entry*

Date	Details	Reference	Dr	Cr
			£	£
	Sales ledger control	GL	98	
	Bank	CB		98
	Removing the incorrect entry: bank receipt for £89 on ...(date)... recorded as £98 instead of £89; in the sales ledger debit L Johnson £98			

Date	Details	Reference	Dr	Cr
			£	£
	Bank	CB	89	
	Sales ledger control	GL		89
	Recording the correct entry: bank receipt for £89 on ...(date)... recorded as £98 instead of £89; in the sales ledger debit L Johnson £89			

10.7

Telephone expenses

Details	Amount £	Details	Amount £
Suspense	210		

Suspense

Details	Amount £	Details	Amount £
Balance b/d	110	Telephone expenses	210
Sales	100		

Sales

Details	Amount £	Details	Amount £
		Suspense	100

Vehicle expenses

Details	Amount £	Details	Amount £
Vehicles	50		

Vehicles

Details	Amount £	Details	Amount £
		Vehicle expenses	50

10.8   (a)   (i)

Account name	Amount £	Debit ✔	Credit ✔
VAT	600	✔	

(ii)

Account name	Amount £	Debit ✔	Credit ✔
VAT	700		✔

(iii)

Account name	Amount £	Debit ✔	Credit ✔
Suspense	100	✔	

(b)   (i)

Account name	Amount £	Debit ✔	Credit ✔
Bank	98	✔	
Vehicle expenses	98		✔

(ii)

Account name	Amount £	Debit ✔	Credit ✔
Vehicle expenses	89	✔	
Bank	89		✔

10.9

Date	Details	Reference	Dr £	Cr £
(a)	Office expenses Suspense *Omission of entry in office expenses account – bank payment made on ....(date)....*	GL GL	85	85
(b)	Suspense Photocopying *Removing the incorrect entry: bank payment for photocopying £87 entered in photocopying account as £78 in error*	GL GL	78	78
	Photocopying Suspense *Recording the correct entry: bank payment for photocopying £87 entered in photocopying account as £78 in error*	GL GL	87	87
(c)	Suspense Sales returns *Overcast on ...(date)... now corrected*	GL GL	100	100
(d)	Commission received Suspense *Commission received on ....(date) entered twice in commission received account, now corrected*	GL GL	25	25

Dr		**Suspense Account**			Cr
20-4		£	20-4		£
30 Sep	Trial balance difference	19	(a)	Office expenses	85
(b)	Photocopying	78	(b)	Photocopying	87
(c)	Sales returns	100	(d)	Commission received	25
		197			197

10.10

Account name	Balances extracted on 31 December 20-4	Balances at 2 January 20-5	
	£	Debit £	Credit £
Office equipment	12,246	12,246	
Bank (debit balance)	3,091	3,091	
Petty cash control	84	84	
Inventory (Stock)	11,310	11,310	
Capital	18,246		18,246
Loan from bank	8,290		8,290
VAT owing to HM Revenue & Customs	3,105		3,105
Purchases ledger control	17,386		17,386
Sales ledger control	30,274	30,274	
Sales	82,410		82,410
Purchases	39,996	*39,496*	
Purchases returns	2,216		2,216
Sales returns	3,471	3,471	
Wages	20,212	20,212	
Advertising	4,300	*4,390*	
Insurance	1,045	1,045	
Heating and lighting	1,237	1,237	
Rent and rates	4,076	4,076	
Postages	721	721	
Suspense account (credit balance)	410		–
Totals		131,653	131,653

Tutorial note: the accounts affected by the journal entries are purchases, advertising and suspense.

10.11

Account name	Balances extracted on 30 April 20-8 £	Balances at 1 May 20-8 Debit £	Balances at 1 May 20-8 Credit £
Sales	101,169		*101,269*
Sales returns	3,476	3,476	
Purchases	54,822	54,822	
Purchases returns	4,107		4,107
Sales ledger control	25,624	25,624	
Purchases ledger control	18,792		18,792
Rent and rates	3,985	3,985	
Advertising	4,867	4,867	
Insurance	1,733	1,733	
Wages	27,391	*31,246*	
Heating and lighting	3,085	3,085	
Miscellaneous expenses	107	107	
Capital	18,171		18,171
Vehicles	22,400	22,400	
Inventory (Stock)	12,454	12,454	
Petty cash control	85	85	
Bank overdraft	6,041		*6,291*
VAT owing to HM Revenue & Customs	3,054		3,054
Loan from bank	12,200		12,200
Suspense account (debit balance)	3,505	–	
Totals		163,884	163,884

Tutorial note: the accounts affected by the journal entries are sales, wages, bank and suspense.

Index